University of South Wales
D0995238

MESSAGE OF A WISE KABOUTER

ROEL VAN DUYN

Translated from the Dutch by
HUBERT HOSKINS

With a Foreword by
CHARLES BLOOMBERG

Dedicated to those who took over the Maagdenhuis.
This is only a beginning

'It is hope, not despair, that makes successful revolutions.'
Kropotkin, *Memoirs of a Revolutionist*

GLAMORGAN POLYTECHNIC
LIBRARY

DUCKWORTH

335.8 DUY
335.83092 DUY
ANARCHISM. SOCIALISM.

First published in Holland by
Meulenhoff Nederland NV, 1969
English translation first published in 1972 by
Gerald Duckworth & Co. Ltd.,
43 Gloucester Crescent, London NW1

© Meulenhoff Nederland NV 1969
English translation © Gerald Duckworth & Co. Ltd
Foreword © Gerald Duckworth & Co. Ltd

All rights reserved

ISBN 0 7156 Cloth 0611 5

ISBN 0 7156 Paper 0632 8

23772

Typeset by Specialised Offset Services Limited, Liverpool

Printed by Unwin Brothers Limited, Old Woking

(31/10/95)

Contents

'Since childhood we have all been taught to regard the State as a kind of providence; our whole upbringing, the Roman history we learnt at school, the Byzantine code which later we studied under the name of Roman law, and the various scientific disciplines which the universities provide, accustom us to believe in the ruling function and the virtues of a new providential State.

To maintain this superstition whole philosophical systems have been elaborated and taught; the whole of politics is based on this principle; and every politician, of whatever complexion, in putting himself forward says to the people: "Give me the power; we can and will release you from the misery that weighs so heavily upon you" '

Kropotkin, *The Conquest of Bread*

Foreword

Roel Van Duyn was born in the Hague in 1943. His mother was a practising theosophist, and his father an accountant who wrote novels. He was educated in a Montessori school, and so grew up in an atmosphere which combined libertarian and mystic ideas. As a teenager, he was greatly influenced by Bertrand Russell, and was expelled from school for leading a ban-the-bomb demonstration. In 1961, he came to Amsterdam University to study history of art and philosophy; there he joined a group of militant anarchists, followers of Domela Nieuwenhuis, the founder of Dutch anarchism. In 1965 he started a magazine, *Provo* (standing for *provocateur*), from which the famous movement took its name. Luud Schimmelpenninck and R. J. Grootveld also helped to found the movement, which staged theatrical happenings round the statue of the Lovable Lad (Lieverdje) in the centre of Amsterdam. The Lovable Lad was donated by a famous tobacco company, and Provo re-christened him 'the enslaved consumer of tomorrow'. Thousands of students, intellectuals and artists joined the movement, which became the archetype of the new-left student rebellions which swept industrialised countries in the late sixties. Its technique was to force authority to reveal the essentially repressive character behind its tolerant, smiling mask. Provo used games, satire and mimicry to undermine the authoritarian personality, as expressed not only in individual behaviour, but also in hierarchic organisations, pyramidal structures and bureaucracies. Its ultimate object was to create unrepressed people – self-actualising, self-reliant, spontaneous, capable of expressing loving feelings and of treating work as play. But clashes with the police earned Provo a name for violence, and the movement reached a climax in 1966, when it disrupted Prince Beatrix's wedding procession with smoke bombs. As an indirect result, Amsterdam's Mayor and Chief of Police were compelled to resign.

Lacking a conventional organisation, the movement began to disintegrate, and wound itself up in 1968. But van Duyn, who survived as the only Provo councillor in Amsterdam's municipal council, continued to develop the implications of Provo thinking. Unhappy at the tendency to violence – one of the Provo groups had called itself the 'desperadoes' – he began to think of ways of turning aggression to creative uses. He came to the conclusion that it was not sufficient only to protest against the alienation and social ills of industrialised consumer society and centralised power. A positive living alternative, a 'realised Utopia', had to be built. Time for mankind being short, what was only possible tomorrow had to be done at once, today.

Van Duyn's vision of this new culture, and the new men who would build it, is set out in the pages of *Message of a Wise Kabouter*, first published in Holland in November 1969, which ran into five editions within a year, and also, in a more personal manner, in *Panic Diary*, which was published in Holland late last year. Both these books are now translated into English for the first time.

The figure which van Duyn chose – the 'kabouter', a gnome or pixie, a fairy-tale figure who lives at the bottom of the garden and speaks to plants and animals – quickly became the badge of a new anarchist-like movement, which set up the Orange Freestate in 1970, 'the alternative society of tomorrow in the world of today'. The name implies not only a political state, but also the state, or condition, of freedom. The Freestate created its own crêches, anti-authoritarian kindergartens, schools, non-poisonous food shops, non-profit-making little industries, and a market. It set up twelve Departments, each parelleling an existing government ministry. The Ministry of Defence in the 'old society' became the Department of Sabotage of Fixed Roles and the Habit of Obedience, whose aim was to create 'an army of responsible dissenters'. The Department of Transport called for flower-gardens on the roofs of cars, which were to be banned from the city centre to reduce pollution. The Department of Housing broke into empty houses and fitted them with plumbing and heating so that homeless people could live there; the Department of Welfare organised a round-the-clock service for old people, emptying dust-bins, buying groceries and reading the Bible at bed-time. Everyone regarded the Freestate as an endearing Alice-in-Wonderland joke. 'A whiff of perfume amid the stale smell of cabbages in our politics,' commented a delighted Premier. But the Gnome idea, with its stress on a more organic way of life and a better relationship with nature, touched a responsive chord in Holland, Europe's most densely populated country. Six months after its formation the Freestate caused a sensation by winning seats in six municipalities. In Amsterdam alone, Pixie candidates won 11 per cent of the vote and five seats on the Council. The Freestate designated its councillors the 'ambassadors of the new society to the old'. All over Europe – in Denmark, Sweden, Belgium, France, Yugoslavia – similar groups were set up. The Freestate withered away at the end of 1971, having failed to fulfil its high expectations, and amid disputes over methods between 'realists' and 'utopians'. But its welfare departments continue. Many members joined militant, semi-autonomous neighbourhood committees, such as the one in the Nieuwmarkt, Amsterdam, which are in the news because of their fierce opposition to new road-building and re-housing schemes. Their tactics include sitting in the branches of trees to prevent city councillors having them cut down.

Van Duyn has now opened a new chapter in the libertarian movement with his latest group, the 'Panic Sowers'. In addition to the common meaning of the word 'panic', he puns on it in two further senses: Pan meaning 'everything', or what is 'universal', and Pan the Greek god of the countryside who defend nature against her enemies. Van Duyn has recently started a journal called 'The Panic Sower', to warn against the imminence of catastrophe caused by growing pollution, war, nationalism and racism. He has also established a Panic University, with correspondence courses in many subjects, including Panicology and Catastrophology.

Van Duyn's outlook is optimistic; he believes in man's goodness and in the capacity of nations to live together peaceably and co-operatively. Today he rejects the dead-end negativism of the Provos; but at the same time he warns of the apocalypse which will overtake the peoples of the world unless they abandon structures which dehumanise them and exploit their neighbours, and instead create societies which allow their innate humanity to flower. Calling for greater scientific responsibility, he believes that it is imperative for technology to be 'cleaned up'.

To his supporters Van Duyn is more priest than politician. Yet, because of his wholesale rejection of traditional politics and its authoritarian principles, he has drawn fire from Right, Left and Centre. He remains a significant phenomenon today because of his appeal to the young and his role during the past decade in fashioning a counter-culture. His writing, however it is regarded, gives a fascinating insight into a major ingredient of today's alternative thought-currents.

Charles Bloomberg
February 1972

PREFACE

Why This Book was Written

In our society, which has become divorced from the real needs of humanity, aggression and the irresponsible use of science are increasing at a terrifying rate. It is tempting to succumb to the kind of pessimism expressed by a friend of mine from Prague, who once said to me: 'You have to feel sorry for Israel, because in a few years' time the Arabs will have atomic bombs, and then the end will be near for every Israeli.' At the time, I replied: 'You have to feel sorry for western civilisation, and for humanity in general, because very soon all countries of any importance will have atomic bombs, and then atomic war will be inevitable. And that means the end of everything.'

On the other hand, in human society as well as in nature, there is a powerful co-operative principle at work to which we and all other creatures owe our existence. Its creative power is such that even in a perverse, panic-stricken and bellicose society, we can survive. We can regard the recent uprisings of the 'provotariat' and of students in the wealthy countries, and the mounting resistance of the exploited proletariat in the poor countries, as signs of hope. They are the first manifestations of a revolution – both national and international, both political and spiritual – which is now approaching fulfilment. This revolution will remove the conditions in which the world is dominated by power-politicians and military leaders, and in which we ourselves are dominated by our own authoritarian tendencies.

The threat of universal annihilation may itself evoke such a revolutionary reaction – this much cybernetics is able to teach us. It is with cybernetics in mind (as I shall show in my final chapter) that I propose to consider the philosophical work of the man who opened my eyes to the significance of co-operation as a factor in evolution, and who, in his own day, had already linked it with the need for a total revolution: Peter Alexandrovitch Kropotkin.

It is the conditional optimism of Kropotkin's philosophy which releases me from despair; and since his message has already been a stimulus to new activity to me, and many others, I do not feel that this book is simply adding to the pointless publications which clutter up our libraries. It is a call to anti-authoritarian activity.

CHAPTER ONE

Kropotkin: a Universal Specialist

Prince Kropotkin was born in 1842, the son of a wealthy Russian landowner. Unaware of his future role as the opponent of exactly this kind of autocrat, he grew up to all appearances in a traditional autocratic mould. At school he was invariably top of his class; and he served as page to Tsar Alexander II. At first, the young Peter Alexandrovitch felt great confidence in this Tsar, who in 1861 had freed the serfs (at least according to the letter of the law). Even as a child, Kropotkin had been touched to the heart by the serfs, being deeply pained at the brutality with which his father treated them.

As a young man in government service, Kropotkin travelled to Siberia and Central Asia, where he made a number of fundamental scientific discoveries. While observing different species of animals, especially rodents, birds and fallow deer, he was surprised to notice that instead of fighting for life among themselves, and competing with one another, they made common cause against their surroundings. That astonished him; for, as a Darwinian and a child of his time, he had expected the opposite. Forty years later, this was to be the starting-point of his main work, *Mutual Aid*. As a geographer, he discovered that the Central Asiatic mountain-range ran not from east to west, as had previously been assumed, but diagonally, from north-east to south-west. On his return to St. Petersburg, he was offered the post of Secretary of the Russian Geographical Society, a distinguished position for a man of his age. But he declined, as a result of another discovery he had made in Siberia. This was the realisation that Tsarism was a monstrous system, to which science ought not to be subjugated. From his own attempts to introduce reforms as an official in Siberia, he had come to see that such reforms were impossible under the regime of the 'Liberator Tsar'. Everything, he concluded, must be changed; and he resolved to dedicate himself to revolution.

In his autobiography, *Memoirs of a Revolutionist*, Kropotkin describes the inner battle he waged before reaching this decision. To throw oneself without restraint into scientific activity seemed to him the finest thing imaginable. 'But what title had I to that exalted joy, when around me I could see nothing but misery and the struggle for a mouldy hunk of bread; when everything that I produced to enable me to remain in that rarified, intellectual world had of necessity to be snatched from the mouths of those who grew the corn and had not bread enough for their children?' Kropotkin here gives expression to a problem which now, a century later, has, alas, only increased in relevance: how can students study without putting themselves, consciously or unconsciously, at the service of a manipulating, war-oriented science and technology?

Later he was to write, in *To the Young*, that once the relisation comes upon one that in a capitalist society science serves the interests only of the ruling class, and keeps the masses in a state of slavery, one stops caring about science for science's sake. One cannot help seeing that a major change is necessary, if science is to be used for good ends. 'You will then look for ways of setting that change in motion; and if you continue to maintain the strict impartiality which governs you in your scientific researches, you will inevitably identify yourself with the cause of socialism, abandon your sophistries, and throw in your lot with us. You will grow tired of working to provide a small group, which already has more than enough, with yet more still; you will put your knowledge and dedication directly at the service of the oppressed.' This is what Kropotkin himself proceeded to do. He joined the *narodniki* as a propagandist for anarchism, of which he was later to become the finest theoretical exponent.

He was arrested and sent to gaol. But, however horrible the reality of Tsarism may have been, its victims were given opportunities to escape which would have been inconceivable under twentieth-century Stalinism. One day during exercise, at a pre-arranged signal (a fiddler playing a mazurka in a nearby inn), he made a run for it and leaped into a carriage driven by friends. Fleeing to the west, he reached Switzerland, where he took and active part in the Bakunist Jura-federation. At first, he supported the anarchist campaign of terror of the eighties, which involved bomb attacks on prominent citizens. Writing in 1879 in his paper, *La Révolte*, he said in a leading article: 'Permanent rebellion expressed through the spoken and written word, the knife, gun, dynamite . . . everything is all right for us, provided it is outside the law' – a maxim resuscitated recently in Fourastier's film, *The Anarchists, or Bonnot's Gang*. This film is a typical example of the stereotyped image of anarchism so often presented by its opponents, as a chaotic faction dedicated to random violence. Why does this cliché persist? No doubt because it gives people such enormous relief to project their suppressed guilt-feelings about the systematic violence of the established order on those who rebel against it. But in actual fact, for the greater part of his life, Kropotkin was against terrorism.

Kropotkin was opposed to any idea of vengeance. In a letter of 1893 he wrote: 'We may say that revenge is not an end in itself. Certainly not. But it is *human*; and all rebellions bear the marks of it and will do so for a long time to come. *We* have not really suffered the kind of persecutions that they, the workers, have had to endure; we, who shut ourselves away in our houses from the cries and sighs of suffering humanity, *we are in no position to judge* those who live amid these hellish privations . . . Personally, I loathe such explosions; but I cannot condemn people who have been driven to despair . . . One thing, however: revenge must not be turned into a *principle*. Nobody has the right to incite others to it; but if he should feel the full smart of all that misery and should commit some desperate act, then let his fellows, those who are pariahs like him, be his judges'.

That, it seems to me, is the attitude we ought to adopt toward the violence now being employed by the *guerilleros* in the Third World. It is easy to say, and is no doubt true, that in the long run, the methods of Gandhi, Luthuli and Martin

Luther King have a greater, and more lasting, effect. But as recipients of Western welfare we are morally obliged to give all the support we can, for example, to the freedom-fighters of Angola in their desperate struggle against sophisticated Portuguese, French, German and American arms, supplied by NATO.

Although his revolutionary activities may never have brought him to the barricades – as did Bakunin's (1814-1876), his predecessor as the intellectual leader of the anarchist movement – Kropotkin did spend long years in prison. Ironically enough, it was he who suffered as scapegoat for the outrages in France. When he entered that country in 1883, planning to give a new stimulus to the movement there, he was arrested with a number of his comrades. On the pretext that they were members of the First International (which was prohibited after the 1871 Paris Commune), they were sentended to five years' imprisonment. 'Cursed be the day when Kropotkin set foot upon the soil of France!' exclaimed the public prosecutor, with the full support of the French government; and the government of Russia, France's ally, awarded him the Cross of St. Anne.

In prison Kropotkin was relatively well treated. Various well-known scholars sent him books; he was free to contribute articles to the *Encyclopaedia Britannica* and *The Nineteenth Century*. Domela Nieuwenhuis, translator of the *Memoirs*, observes enviously that he was allowed everything, in sharp contrast to her own treatment in Utrecht prison. His wife was allowed in every day. 'What is more', recalls Kropotkin in the *Memoirs*, 'we worked a narrow strip of land running beside the wall, and within the space of eighty square ells we grew almost incredible amounts of lamb's lettuce and radishes, as well as some flowers. Needless to say, we at once set up classes for study; and during the three years I spent at Clairvaux I gave my companions lessons in geography, mathematics and physics, and helped them with their languages.'

Kropotkin did not serve his full five years. By pressure of international sympathy, especially from intellectuals (Herbert Spencer and Victor Hugo, for instance, signed a petition for his release), he was set free in 1886. He settled in London, and established himself there as a universal writer. Besides his chief work, *Mutual Aid*, his publications included an outstanding work on the French Revolution; a survey of Russian literature in the nineteenth century; a book (*Fields, Factories and Workshops*) on the integration of industry and agriculture, and of mental and physical labour; and *The Conquest of Bread*, a vision of society as it might be after the revolution. He also published articles in *The Nineteenth Century* on geographical subjects.

In London he was a popular figure: English publications continually refer to him as 'the saintly Kropotkin'. He had many friends, not only among scientists (though at their meetings he alone refused to raise his glass to Queen Victoria), but also among working people, to whom he expounded the rich possibilities of a society with the minimum of coercion. He gave innumerable lectures, and founded the anarchist weekly, *Freedom*, which still appears today. He lived there as one who 'overflows with ideas; he scatters them by the handful. He is distressed if he cannot spread them and sow them everywhere; life for him is simply that.' Those are his own words (in *An Independent Morality*); and they convey an unconscious self-portrait. To me, as I picture Kropotkin, with his luxuriant beard, working away in his garden and admiring the unity of man and nature, he appears a wise gnome, a 'kabouter' whose message the world still fails to understand.

Let me now give a brief survey of Kropotkin's political ideas. (His philosophy of mutual aid will be dealt with later.)

Kropotkin saw the capitalist society of his day as a two-headed monster. One head was its authoritarian structure, the other the wages-system. The structure was authoritarian in that a small ruling section, composed of representatives of the interests of capital, enacted laws and determined national policy for millions of people. A nation had no effective control over 'its' government because it was deprived of the instruments of power and information. It had insufficient opportunity to develop its own initiatives in free co-operation, being obstructed by the one-sided laws established by the government. Authority acted as a brake on free development. It would do man no harm – indeed it would give him pleasure – to dispense with authority. By consultation and reciprocal agreements, we could arrive at a voluntary co-operation that would give us infinitely more satisfaction in work. Co-operation without coercion must also eventually increase the pace of development, because people work better and more quickly when they are doing something of their own free will; and also because free collaboration between people would put an end to the unequal distribution of wealth and education, so that many more people could be involved in intellectually-demanding work. Man was not as bad as some would have us believe. The myth of the fall aroused in people a cringing feeling of guilt and made them submit to authority. As he said in *After the Revolution: No Judges, No Prisons*, 'Belief in the necessity of an authoritarian constitution for society is merely superstition, artificially bred and systematically instilled into the public'.

All our lives we are told that authority is essential. Without authority the world would be chaos: this is the message we learn everywhere – at school, at university, on the street, from employers, in the newspapers, on television. Alas, the evidence for this claim is weak indeed. Is the present world chaos due to a lack of authority? Who is on the verge of atomic, bacteriological or chemical warfare which will destroy the world for good – the governments of the USA and Russia, or the anti-authoritarian students? the powerful directors of armament factories and other aggressive industries, or the common people of the world who have no power?

Everything points to the view that, thanks to the authoritarian organization of society, it is those who wield power who are responsible for abuses. It is authority that threatens us. There is no evidence at all to support the false but current notion that, without authority, things would disintegrate further. On the contrary, it seems clear that societies not based on authority create a type of person less open to its abuse, because from an early age they have learnt (not by indocrination but by developing their natural gifts) how to co-operate with others, instead of ruling or obeying, and how to be responsible for others and for themselves. Fear holds us back from freedom. As Kropotkin says in *The Morality of Anarchism*, 'We are not afraid to say: "Do what you will, behave as you will"; for we are convinced that the great majority of mankind, according to the degree of understanding they have reached and the completeness with which they have thrown off their chains, will behave and act in a way beneficial to society; just as we are confident in advance that one day a child will stand on two feet, instead of four, simply because it has been born of parents who belong to the species *homo sapiens*'.

But Kropotkin was not wholly right when he declared that authority was based only on superstition. He thought it could maintain itself only by oppression and deceit on the part of those in power, who were the successors to earlier 'sorcerers, rainmakers, miracle-workers, priests, people with special knowledge of ancient customs and the leaders of warlike hordes', who forced the people to acknowledge their supremacy. But why were they so often successful? I cannot believe that it was simply credulity. Underlying man's credulity is his tendency to build socicty hicrarchically. Anyone who fails to consider the catastrophic consequences of authoritarian power is all too ready to resign himself to it. One of man's characteristics is his almost universal fear of finding himself in the dark. This irrational fear, with which we are all familiar, sets up a need for some fixed authority, for laws that will 'protect' us. The fear within us, and the need for hierarchy which it reinforces, are the father and mother, so to speak, of the credulity which the mass of people show toward authority. How are we to come to terms with this 'father and mothcr' without becoming their victims? Only by being rational enough to gratify the equally irrational and powerful need within us for freedom; by creating an anti-authoritarian society, in which the fear will not be further stimulated by what are at present the very real dangers of war and famine, and in which the need for hierarchy will be satisfied. There would still be a rudimentary hierarchy in this society, but it would be adaptable, and would have eliminated the sharp contrasts that at present exist between millionaires and the starving, between those who control atomic forces and the defenceless, many of whom are illiterate. Its functions, which would alter with every change in society, would be carried out by elected representatives of various groups, replaced by others at short intervals, and at all times answerable to their electors.

For Kropotkin, therefore, revolution does not mean that a different group of rulers assumes power and maintains the old authoritarian structure under a different banner. It was his great merit (as it was of Bakunin and the other anarchists) to have exposed in advance the specious, pseudo-socialistic character of the Soviet government before it ever came to power. Kropotkin knew, in any case, that a revolution cannot be run by a single group. 'The conspirators who persist in their bias toward dictatorship are in that way unconsciously working to bring their enemies to power.' Trotsky, after his downfall, had to admit that his enemies had gained power. A government cannot be revolutionary, declared Kropotkin, it can only be more or less monopolistic. 'In order to meet the many diverse conditions and needs that will arise as an immediate consequence of the abolition of private property, everyone must work together. Any external authority can only be an obstacle to the organic task that has to be accomplished, and at the same time a source of hatred and dissension.' What ought to happen after the revolution? Kropotkin tried to expound this in *The Conquest of Bread*. Not without some diffidence; for like other anarchist theoreticians, he started from the conviction that it was impossible, and wrong in principle, to plan comprehensively for a complete society, because it must be left to people in the circumstances of the actual revolution to experiment with their own ideas. He merely offered a guide line.

Kropotkin's new society was based on anarchistic communism. This had almost nothing in common with the sort of communism that is in power in fourteen countries today. Kropotkin would have described that as state socialism or authoritarian communism. Anarchistic communism had to do with the collective ownership of both the means of production and consumer articles. 'From each according to his ability, to each according to his need' would be the norm. Ownership of the means of production would be abolished. The workers would be responsible for their factories;

students, scientists and staff for their universities and schools. Worker and student councils would send their delegates to local councils, which would also uphold consumer interests. Representatives of the local councils would form regional councils, and representatives of the regions national councils. In this way the world would be a federation of encompassed communes, while each commune in itself would be a federation of individuals. Nor did Kropotkin see the commune as indissolubly tied to a stretch of territory: his notion of it was much broader. 'For us the "commune" is no longer a territorial agglomeration; it is more of a generic term, a snynonym for the grouping of peers who know no frontiers or barriers. The social commune will soon cease to be a sharply demarcated entity. Each group in the commune will necessarily become involved with other corresponding groups in other communes; they will be conjoined and federated with them, with links just as strong as those uniting them with their fellow citizens – and that will set up a community of interests, the members of which are dispersed among thousands of towns and villages.' Kropotkin saw this trend as already present in society, in the many scientific, literary and sporting organizations, and in the international railway and postal unions.

What was new about anarchistic communism was that each person would be paid not according to his performance but according to his need; and that lopped off the second head of the monster capitalism – namely, the wages system. Because it is impossible to determine the contribution of this or that individual in the ever more complicated process of production, it is impossible to pay a just wage, which Bakunin and the Marxists still wanted to do. Anarchistic communism was the novel contribution that Kropotkin as a political theoretician made to socialism. The idea was invented by French communards and Italian anarchists, but Kropotkin was the first to develop and propagate it in a systematic way. 'Individual appropriation is neither just nor practicable. Everything belongs to everybody. All things are for all people, because all need and require them, because all people according to their capability have worked in order to produce them and because it is not possible to determine each person's share in the production of the world's wealth . . . All is for each and every one!' But if everyone could take as much as he wanted, wouldn't his acquisitiveness lead him to take more than he needed? To this objection Kropotkin replied that the principle of free consumption was already to some extent being applied in capitalist society, and that it worked even here. When you take a tram, the price of your ticket, in most countries, is irrespective of the number of stages you wish to ride in the vehicle; yet nobody is going to ride too far just to get his full money's worth. If you insure yourself, you usually do so against a fixed premium which is independent of the size of the total amount that the insurance may eventually yield; within limits, the sum total can vary quite a bit. When a house catches fire, the fire-brigade always comes, no matter how much or little the occupier may have done to benefit society and deserve its help. When ships are in danger off the coast, the rescue services do not ask for compensation in case of loss before turning out: the fact that the sufferers are human beings is reason enough in itself, without expectation of payment. Up to a point, the principle of free consumption is also applied nowadays to the use of roads, streets, water, air, parks, libraries and so on.

Insofar as it is applied in capitalist society, free consumption is deficient, not only because it is insufficiently widespread, but because it depends on a fixed monetary payment, rather than on the work which everyone performs for himself and for society. Another deficiency, Kropotkin said, is that the consumer has no voice in the running of various businesses. In a society in which there are shortages, anarchist communism cannot function properly. When demand exceeds supply, goods have to be rationed. Kropotkin reckoned that an anarcho-communist society would soon succeed in establishing a flourishing economy, allowing for the growth of free consumption. As soon as people realised that there was always enough in the shops, they would stop taking more than they required for their immediate needs. If they once took too much of something, they would soon have had enough; and a rational economy backed by the most modern means of production would easily be able to bear the loss. One might add that the system would have to be introduced by slow stages. Vandalism, a form of aggression touched off by capitalist society with its inherent tension between artifically fostered demands and specious consumer articles, must first have a chance to die away in a truly socialist environment. Kropotkin made it clear that the difficulties encountered in a capitalist economy were due not to overproduction but to underconsumption. It was only because the proletarians (at that time the European working-class, now the ordinary people of the Third World) had no money to buy things with, that the economy failed to function properly, and not – as has frequently been asserted – because too much was produced, although this argument is still used as justification for destroying 'overproduced' foodstuffs.

Kropotkin concluded that on a reasonable reckoning, the primary requisites for each family could be produced in 150 five-hour working days, and the secondary ones like wine, furniture, transport, in a further 150 such days. And how much briefer again, with our present machinery of production, might we not render the whole process! By the technical perfecting of production, automation removes the final argument against free consumption. We might have to set a limit to our consumption for the time being, because we are bound to give so much in the way of food, equipment and services to the poor countries; but even that restriction could be dropped after a few decades.

Kropotkin understood that luxury was a precondition of a happy society. Once bread had been assured, the chief goal would be leisure. 'Man is not a being whose sole purpose is to eat, drink and provide himself with lodging. As soon as his material needs have been met, other needs present themselves which can be described in general terms as of an artistic character. These needs are very diverse, varying from individual to individual; and the more highly developed a society is, the more will individuality be unfolded and the more diversified will people's wants become.' Kropotkin thus did not make the mistake of regarding man's needs and demands as static, as one might perhaps conclude from his maxim 'from each according to his ability, to each according to his need'.

In *Fields, Factories and Workshops*, Kropotkin worked out an economy and ecology aimed at expediting the emergence of a complete human being in an autonomous community. He was against job-specialisation and industrial specialisation by regions, because it would render people unnecessarily one-sided and myopic. What he aimed at was the creation of the universal specialist – although he did not use that term.

Kropotkin was opposed to the views of Adam Smith and his followers. 'Till now, political economy has put the main emphasis on *distribution*. We advance the case for *integration*; and we maintain that the model for a society – that is, the situation toward which society is already moving – is a society of combined, integrated labour – a society in which each individual is productive of physical as well as mental work; in which every healthy human being works, and every worker works on the land as well as in industry; in which every group of individuals big enough to command a certain variety of natural resources – it could be a nation or more likely a region – itself manufactures and uses most of its own agricultural and industrial products.'

This does not mean that he was opposed to the exchange of goods. On the contrary, interchange of scientific insights, ideas, culture and material products must be extended even further. He merely wished to prevent regions and countries from dependence on others and from an ill-balanced economy. He wanted to decentralise agriculture and industry so that factory gates and workshops looked on to cultivated land, and gardens extended into the towns. Later, a whole school of regionalists such as Geddes and Mumford, and garden-city experimenters such as Ebenezer Howard, tried to elaborate this idea. Auroville, the yogi-town in India which is built in the form of a Milky Way, is similar. The gardens of Auroville run in between the built-up spiralling arms of the city as far as the centre; a paradise compared with the technocratic rubbish-heaps that we call towns. But so long as there continues to be a club of wealthy countries which concentrate on industry and content themselves with exploiting the poor countries' raw materials, monocultures will continue to be a natural symptom of a sick global economy with sick global cities.

If they are to attain complete integration of their capacities, children must be given an integral upbringing. They must not be taken passively on a partial tour of knowledge until they become myopic specialists. Kropotkin's 'integral education' was aimed at providing children both with expertise and with scientific understanding. Especially in the age of automation, that is a precondition of democracy. How are we to prevent the emergence of a small, omnipotent class of computer specialists, except by teaching as many people as possible about machines?

At the end of *Fields, Factories and Workshops*, Kropotkin predicted that, if and when his plans were put into practice, technology and science would so reduce the time needed for producing the desired degree of prosperity, whatever that was, that everybody would have as much leisure as they wanted. 'They (technology and science) cannot guarantee happiness, of course; for happiness depends as much – or even more – on the individual himself as on his environment. But they do at least guarantee the happiness that is to be found in the comprehensive and varied exercise of the diverse capacities of a human being, in work which does not have to be a chore and in the awareness that one is not trying to build one's own good fortune on other people's misery.'

Kropotkin's life was a long one. At the outbreak of the First World War, which he had seen coming, he was forced to declare his position. He who had struggled all his life against nationalism and militarism now felt himself compelled to opt for one or other of the warring parties. For France, in fact: for a France whose revolutionary tradition he so much admired – and against Germany whose conservatism he abhorred. It is a pity that Kropotkin failed to follow the example of Bakunin, who in 1870 issued a call to a revolutionary people's war against both France and Germany, or of Lenin, who did the same during the First World War. It would have given his life a greater consistency and would have increased rather than detracted from his influence in revolutionary circles. As it was, Stalin was able to say of him, not entirely without reason: 'The old fool must have lost his head completely'.

Many anarchists, including Errico Malatesta, Domela Nieuwenhuis, Emma Goldman, Alexander Berkman and Rudolf Rocker, turned from him in disappointment. Trotsky, in his *History of the Russian Revolution* could write of him with some spite: 'The superannuated anarchist, Kropotkin, who from his early days always had a soft spot for the *Narodniks*, made use of the war to disavow what he had been teaching for almost half a century. This indicter of the State supported the Entente . . .' But Kropotkin regarded the impending German victory as a world catastrophe which had to be prevented at all costs. A catastrophe it certainly would have been; but did it necessitate support of France? In 1917, to Kropotkin's great joy, came the long-awaited Russian revolution. In 1905, he had wanted to go to Russia, during the first, abortive revolution, and he had even taught himself to use a rifle for the purpose, but circumstances had prevented him. Now, at the age of 75, he hurried away from London to his native land.

In St. Petersburg he was welcomed by an enormous crowd. A military band played the Marseillaise. But the anarchists were absent. Regretfully, the old anti-militarist considered it his first duty to summon the war-weary Russians to enlist against the Germans, with the result that he found himself politically isolated. He was alienated, on the one hand, from the anarchitsts, who like the bolsheviks had a programme of peace and immediate social revolution. On the other hand, he had no use for Kerensky, who invited him to take part in his government, because logically enough he still saw state and government as evils. As he said in *Revolutionary Government*: 'Nothing is good and enduring except what arises out of the free initiative of the people; and every government has a tendency to kill this. Even the best among us, therefore, would be ripe for the scaffold within a week, should they ever become masters of that mighty machine: the government that permits them to act as they please.'

In February 1918, the Bolsheviks, taking counter-revolutionary activity as a pretext, began to persecute and arrest the anarchists. Kropotkin was reconciled with them, but it was too late. Even conversations between Kropotkin and Lenin – who tried to placate him to get his support –

came to nothing. Civil war led to the violation of every human right. The Bolsheviks even revived the practice of taking hostages. Kropotkin wrote passionately to Lenin that this was a return to the darkest periods of history: 'If you consent to such methods, one can foresee that one day you will start using torture, as in the Middle Ages. How can you, Vladimir Ilyich, you who wish to be the apostle of new verities and the builder of a new state, accede to such a repellent policy, to such unacceptable methods? Such a measure is the equivalent of saying that you openly admit that you support the ideas of yesterday . . . Are you so blind, so much the prisoner of your authoritarian ideas, that you fail to realise that, being now at the head of European communism, you do not have the right to defile the ideas you uphold by using discreditable means, means which are proof not only of a monstrous error but also of an unwarranted fear for your own life? What future is there for communism when one of its principal champions tramples like this over all decent feelings?'

As Kropotkin was an internationally respected embodiment of the socialist revolution, Lenin's government dared not imprison him. Tucked away in the remote village of Dmitrov, he was left unmolested. Here he wrote his last book, *Ethics*, which he never finished. Here too he wrote his last political pamphlet, his *Letter to the Workers of the Western World.* He called upon them to boycott the intervention of the western powers in Russia, and to demand an end to the blockade: 'All armed intervention from abroad necessarily strengthens the dictatorial proclivities of the government, and paralyses the efforts of those Russians who, independently of the government, are prepared to assist Russia in the restoration of her life . . . The evil inherent in state communism is increased tenfold by the argument that all our misery is caused by foreign intervention. I must also point out that if military intervention by the Allies continues, this will certainly generate in Russia a feeling of bitterness toward the western nations, a sentiment that will be exploited in the event of future conflicts . . . In short, it is high time that the European nations entered into direct relations with Russia.' In his letter Kropotkin refers to the original idea of the Soviets, the autonomous workers' councils, as 'magnificent', because they would lead to direct participation by the actual producers in the work-process. But the lack of a free press, and of free elections for the workers' and peasants' councils, reduced them to the status of passive instruments of the party dictatorship. In the conclusion, he predicts a great future for socialism, when the workers will institute a new International, independent of any political party, which will make direct collaboration possible between the various peoples.

At the beginning of 1921, when the Kronstadt Commune, which was completely in agreement with Kropotkin's ideas, was suppressed, and the guerilla forces in the Ukraine of the anarchist leader, Machno, were put down by Trotsky, Kropotkin died. At the moment of his death his son-in-law saw a dazzling green comet with a long tail shoot across the sky – symbol of the departure of a universal revolutionary.

It is sometimes said that Kropotkin's funeral was the last occasion the Russian anarchists were free inside Russia. The truth is sadder still. The Bolshevik government meant to do all it could to make a favourable impression on the nation, and especially on foreign journalists. They offered a state funeral, with full honours, which Kropotkin's family and friends refused. Kameniev undertook to release all the imprisoned anarchists to enable them to attend. But in spite of this, on the day of the funeral only seven of the thousands of anarchists were set free, although Kameniev repeated his promise when he was telephoned by an indignant funeral-committee. At the last minute, the authorities mistrusted the spirit of Kropotkin. Victor Serge, who was there, tells us: 'The shadow of the Cheka was everywhere; but the crowd was large and sympathetic . . . With his stern countenance, smooth, high forehead, sculptured nose and snow-white beard, Kropotkin resembled a sleeping prophet, while around him angry voices were whispering that the Cheka had broken Kameniev's promise . . . The black flags, the speeches, the fearful whispering lashed the crowd into a frenzy . . .'

CHAPTER TWO

As it is Above, so it is Below

In the nineteenth century, imperialism, competition and aggression were not indulged, as they are in the twentieth, with fine-sounding pretexts. Even in liberal Britain – or rather precisely there – they were officially and openly supported by scientific theory. In 1793, William Godwin, the father of modern anarchism, declared in his *Enquiry Concerning Political Justice* that it should be possible to create universal prosperity with minimal effort, if the potentialities of science were exploited and all harmful social activities, such as war, avoided. This view of science, held by the liberal bourgeoisie, was answered by a cleric, T.H. Malthus. There was a natural tendency, Malthus said, for population to increase faster than food-production. Total famine could be prevented only by 'positive checks' such as natural disasters, periodic famines, wars, and a permanent competitive struggle in which the weaker inevitably lost. The resulting sacrifice of minorities was the only way to prevent the total destruction of mankind. It was criminal, therefore, to counter or forestall these 'positive checks'. Unrestricted competition was vital to the human species; any attempt to change the situation was useless and could lead only to greater misery. This untenable theory was refuted by Godwin and Hazlitt in their *Reply to Malthus*, in which they showed that Malthus's calculations were incorrect. But for the politicians, generals and industrialists Malthus's idea was too good an argument to lay aside. They went on maintaining it; and the theory still survives, especially in its application to the Third World, even though, fortunately, our scientists would not now dare to proclaim it publicly.

Malthus had a great influence on Darwin, who helped to lay the ideological foundations of nineteenth-century capitalism. In the *Origin of Species* (1859), Darwin argued that animals and human beings, if freely permitted to propagate their kind, multiply in a geometrical progression. But nature maintains an equilibrium: on average, there is a constant number of individuals of any particular species. There must, therefore, be a big mortality rate, indicating that individuals are bound to engage in a hard 'struggle for life'. Darwin explained the great variation in exemplars of a species by the 'survival of the fittest', or 'natural selection'. And so Malthus's 'positive checks' took on a continuing life in a subtler guise.

The struggle for life can be interpreted in two ways: as a struggle against natural circumstances, or as a conflict of living creatures among themselves. Darwin himself, and more especially his disciple, T.H. Huxley, put the emphasis on mutual struggle and competition. Darwin went so far as to say that competition was a moral imperative, if degeneration was to be prevented. In the *Descent of Man* (1871) we read: 'Like any other animal, man has undoubtedly ascended to his present high level by means of a struggle for existence resulting from his rapid production; and if he is to advance yet higher still, one fears that he must remain subject to a bitter struggle. He would otherwise relapse into indolence, and the more gifted would have no more success in the battle for life than the less gifted. Thus our natural rate of reproduction, althouh it will lead to many and obvious difficulties, should in no event be greatly diminished. There must be free competition for all human beings.'

It is understandable that employers and financiers should be overjoyed at these words, and should agree wholeheartedly when Darwin says that the 'civilised races' will inevitably soon stamp out the 'savage races' and will usurp their territory. In his autobiography, Darwin expressed great admiration for Huxley. Huxley had already adopted a negative attitude to Kropotkin, even before the publication of *Mutual Aid*, in which Kropotkin contested Huxley's ideas on evolution. Indeed Huxley had been one of the few intellectuals who refused to sign the petition for Kropotkin's release from Clairvaux gaol. In his *Struggle for Life Manifesto* (1889), Huxley compared the animal kingdom, ethically speaking, with a gladiatorial show, since 'the strongest, the fleetest and the most cunning stay alive for the next day's fight. The spectator has no need to turn his thumb down; for no quarter is given.'

In the new science of anthropology, there was a revival of the influence of the seventeenth-century philosopher Thomas Hobbes. Hobbes taught that when there is no strong ruler at the head of the state, a war of every man against every other is inevitable. The ruler, who owes his position to men's fears of one another, decides the law. In the state of nature in which primitive peoples live, there is no state and no law; and so every man is at war with his neighbour, because in relation to each other, men are essentially like wolves: *homo homini lupus.*

The nineteenth-century bourgeoisie, therefore, had no lack of justifying arguments for their exploitation, subjugation and massacre of the proletariat and coloured races. If Karl Marx has the credit for undermining the economic foundations of laisser-faire liberalism, it was Kropotkin who, in his *Mutual Aid*, refuted the biological and anthropological arguments for it, and thus destroyed its philosophical basis as well.

In fact, Kropotkin actually quoted with approval Hobbes' *homo homini lupus.* But he showed, with a flood of persuasive examples, that all animals – including wolves – evince a social character, and help each other. According to him, this means that if authority were to be removed, people would not attack each other; instead, spontaneous co-operation would emerge. The principal factor in evolution is not competition or mutual conflict, but mutual aid. 'Do not compete! Competition is always bad for the species and there are enough ways to avoid it!' This is the way of nature, though not always fully realised. The watchword that comes to us from the woods, the forest, the river, the ocean, is: 'Unite – help one another! That is the surest way to provide the greatest security for each and all, the best guarantee of existence and progress, physical, intellectual and moral.'

In the early chapters of *Mutual Aid*, Kropotkin shows us

how almost all animals co-operate in one way or another in hunting, fishing, singing, dancing, playing, protecting their young and themselves, migrating and nesting. Remarkably enough, he bases his argument on Darwin's idea that the struggle for existence and natural selection are the central concepts of evolution; but he interprets the struggle for existence as a struggle not between competing individuals, but against the hostile conditions encountered by different groups and species from birth in their natural surroundings. Darwin himself had already said in the *Origin of Species* that he envisaged the term 'struggle for life' figuratively, as the following passage shows (Chapter 3): 'I must say at once that I am using the term "struggle for existence" in a general and figurative sense, to include the dependence of one creature upon another and to include (what is more important) not only the life of the individual but success in leaving progeny. Of two rodents in a period of scarcity it really can be said that they fight together over which is going to obtain food and life. But of a plant on the edge of a desert one can say that it wages a battle for life against the drought, although one should really say that it is dependent on humidity . . . In these various senses, which run into one another, for the sake of convenience I shall use the general term "struggle for existence".'

But later, he and his disciples appear to have forgotten this. Modern biologists agree with Kropotkin that the struggle for existence must be understood in a figurative sense. Furthermore, Kropotkin pointed out how wrong was Darwin's Malthusian hypothesis that there had to be ruthless competition in nature in order to account for the contrast between (*a*) the relatively constant number of individuals which he observed, and (*b*) the increase of individuals in a geometrical progression which he foresaw in theory, if no obstacles were placed in the way of the reproductive process. Kropotkin argued that obstacles consist not so much in reciprocal competition as in the lethal conditions presented by the natural environment. Eggs are destroyed on a massive scale by storm and flood, and also because they are used by animals as food. Many living animals die of hunger, cold, heat, drought and disease. On this point, modern science supports Kropotkin. In the struggle for existence against a hostile environment, natural selection works to prevent competition as much as possible. 'Ants', Kropotkin points out, 'get together in nests and tribes; they hoard their provisions, they rear 'cattle' (ingeniously exploiting greenfly) – and so they eschew competition; and natural selection picks out from the ant families those kinds that best understand the skill of avoiding competition, with its inevitably baneful consequences. Most northern birds gradually migrate southwards as winter comes; or they flock together and set out on long journeys – thus avoiding competition. Many rodents go to sleep when the season approaches in which competition might arise; while others build up stocks of food for the winter and combine into large villages in order to have sufficient protection when they are at work. Reindeer move to the sea when the lichens have dried up inland. Bison will travel across a vast continent to find food. And beavers, when they become too numerous on a river, divide into two groups, the elders moving downsteam, the youngsters upstream. Competition is avoided. If the animals do not hibernate or migrate or build up their food stocks or even cultivate their food like the ants, they behave like the titmice and simply turn to new kinds of food – a habit charmingly described by Wallace in his *Darwinism* – and so once more competition is avoided.'

Thus Kropotkin points to aspects of nature, and of Darwin's work, completely different from those stressed by his liberal contemporaries, who called a thing 'bestial' when they meant 'cruel, anti-social, depraved'. It was the weak he saw as playing the major role in evolution and in the improvement of a species. The 'bruisers', those who feel no immediate necessity for co-operation because they think they can rely on themselves and their muscles, were outstripped and died out sooner than more fragile but more social animals. The dinosaurs, in fact, had perished, whereas the ants flourished more than ever and of all earth's creatures had least cause to worry about their future. It was the weak who felt themselves most obliged to co-operate and to be artful.

To lend force to his argument, Kropotkin asks his readers to note that Darwin understood very well the social character of man. He quotes from the *Descent of Man*: 'Man's limited muscular strength, his slow gait, his lack of natural weapons, etc. are more than compensated for, in the first place, by his intellectual capacities [which, Kropitkin emphasises, Darwin also sees as acquired mainly for the purpose of furthering life in society]; and secondly, by his social qualities, which induce him to give aid to his fellows and receive it from them.' From this interesting passage it can be inferred that Darwin was indeed aware of man's social character, but in conformity with the spirit of the age was not prepared to see as much in it as Kropotkin and some modern theorists.

Remarkably enough, in all this the materialist Kropotkin is in agreement with the priest Teilhard de Chardin. Kropotkin considers the brain to be a social endowment *par excellence*, especially in humans. Teilhard believes that progress in evolution can be gauged by the slowly but surely increasing complexity of the brain, which he calls the 'law of cephalization'. The development of mind presupposes an increasing degree of co-operation. The resulting socialization imbues men with a greater and greater awareness that they must rely upon working together. Teilhard, like Kropotkin, anticipates that more and more intense co-operation and socialization will release people from material anxieties, and that the flowering of a full-scale democratic art and science will become possible. The various races will get together and be integrated. Both believe that if an *Ubermensch* – a superman – does emerge, it will be as a consequence of a sublime socialization, making a real individualisation possible.

Kropotkin would have been delighted by a model of the hydrogen atom. An electron moves round the proton that forms the nucleus precisely as the moon circles the earth and the earth the sun. The parallel would have strengthened his confidence that nature is a unity; for essentially Kropotkin is the magician-like figure one sees depicted on the highest card of the Tarot pack, with one arm pointing upward and the other downward. As it is above, so it is below. As it is in nature, so is it in culture. As it is with the life of animals, so is it with that of human kind. Every bird may be told by its note; but in substance its song is always the same. Psychologists are right to relate their study of human beings more and more to results obtained from the study of animals, though they should not forget that every bird is distinct and separate and sounds a note of its own.

Perhaps it will be said that it is entirely unnecessary to demonstrate that mutual aid and co-operation constitute the motive force in nature because, even if that were not the case, it would still be a dire necessity for human beings to work together; or it may be said that affection between human beings is necessary and desirable because that is what we want, and not because of an analogy with nature. I am afraid that those who argue in this way overestimate the ability of the human will to disengage itself from universal patterns.

In *The Naked Ape*, Desmond Morris has amply demonstrated that *homo sapiens* is the one hundred and ninety-third species of ape, though in the course of his existence he has developed very special faculties which have enabled him to construct a culture extraneous to the animal world. Why are the correspondences in the social organisation of men and apes and wolves so obvious? The reason is that man is a predator who has within him the characteristic traits of both ape and wolf. When, for some geographical reason, the primate from which man originated was forced out of his initial environment, the primeval forest, and found himself in the savannah, he was obliged to give up his ape-like existence – vegetarian, foraging and nomadic. From predators such as wolves he took over the practice of hunting in co-operative groups of males, as well as meat-eating and the occupying of a particular territory. In order to be able to compete with much more heavily armoured predators, the naked ape was compelled to make artificial weapons. (This is an instance of competition between species, which would seem to be fiercer than competition between members of a species.) The manufacturing and use of tools marked the beginning of an imposing culture, with which the culture of the ants offered only a pale comparison, although its complex organisation, which included building, agriculture and cattle-rearing, had already existed for a long time. I cannot believe that from the moment he began to construct his culture man ceased to be part of nature. I would be unable to believe it, even without the evidence of Desmond Morris, or of biologists like Portmann, who affirms that the number of hereditary co-ordinates which help to determine our behaviour is no less than with the higher animals; or of all the mystics and philosophers, from the ancient Indians to Spinoza, who have pointed to the unity and cohesion of everything that exists.

Is it likely that we are alien meteors, as it were, flung down here on the earth by gods beyond the universe as having nothing in common with terrestrial nature? Is it not already obvious enough how mortally dangerous it is for us to upset the biological equilibrium? The fact that, as the astronomers tell us, there are millions of planets in the universe compatible with the earth, suggests that there exist beings to whom we bear a still closer resemblance than we do to the non-human creatures on earth. What an arrogant and stupid idea to think that man is unique in Creation!

Behaviour patterns in nature must surely be full of ethical and philosophical significance for us. If it is true, as Kropotkin says, that blind pelicans are fed by their sighted companions, and that such behaviour among them is the rule rather than the exception, then surely there is at least a chance that in men also the urge to co-operate will be great enough to enable them to surmount the dangers of atomic war and environmental pollution.

The progress of biological and physical research since Kropotkin's day has corroborated his view that reciprocal co-operation has been a dominating factor in evolution. Co-operation starts as far back as the inorganic stage. Through the forces of gravity and electrical attraction (forces which are comparable at the organic level with the social instinct), freely rotating electrons and protons combine to form atoms. Atoms combine with one another to release energy; and in this way 'life' (in the narrower sense) becomes possible. On our sun, for example, hydrogen atoms continually combine to form helium gas. Everything combines: in 'inanimate' nature molecules continually do so.

S.T. Bok, in *The Emergence of Life*, comes to the conclusion that all properties which are regarded as characterising life also occur in the largest norm-conditioned entities in a cooling star. Norm-conditioned entities are delimited, structured units of matter, moving freely through space. For matter is not continuous, but is of its nature divided into norm-conditioned or standardised units which combine with one another. These particles exhibit the typical features of life: differentiation, reproduction, mutation, individuality, metabolism or the circulation of matter, and probably also reactive coupling. The mutual aid which the combining particles afford each other consists in the metabolic process which releases energy and thus – to the advantage of the particles themselves – makes life possible.

Professor van Melsen, in his *Evolution*, also reaches a Kropotkinian conclusion: 'The main factor [in evolution] is the natural affinity of certain compounds, enabling them to combine into more complex, stable structures. The biochemist thinks and experiments on the basis of those affinities. Similarly, only those mutations play a role in the life process that yield viable total structures. The possible routes for evolution are therefore determined by structures and not by fortuitous agglomerations in themselves.' Not only the process of combining, but the process of splitting entails a relationship of mutual dependence. When the nucleus of the amoeba divides in order to reduplicate itself, the daughter nucleus remains for a considerable time in the amoeba's protoplasm. Every change affecting the protoplasm will evoke a shared response on the part of the mother- and daughter-cells. There is a complete interchange of physiologically necessary substances between mother-cell and daughter-cell so long as they remain situated within the same membrane. The one is dependent on the other. And this principle obviously holds good not only for dividing amoebas but for all pregnant female creatures in general.

When it comes to reproduction, the mutual dependence of living organisms finds particularly striking expression. The sperm is dependent on the ovum, the ovum on the sperm, the offspring on its mother, the mother on her offspring, man on woman, woman on man. It looks as though nature, in her representational, creative power, wanted to hold these up to us as symbols of the mutual dependence and interconnectedness of all things.

As Kropotkin had already pointed out, Darwin (the 'other' Darwin) had remarked in the *Descent of Man* that those animal species with the greatest number of individuals displaying mutual solidarity have the best chance of staying alive and of acquiring abundant offspring. A biologist of our own day, Warder Allee, has done laboratory work that supports this view. In his *Co-operation Among Animals with Human Implications*, he concludes that in all the various branches of the animal kingdom, from protozoa to insects and men, safety to some extent increases, the greater the number of exemplars congregated together. For many animals the group affords protection against heat and cold. Take the emperor penguins, for example, who live at the south pole in temperatures of 25 to 35 degrees below zero and in snow-storms of 130 kilometers per hour. To conserve energy, they eschew any kind of aggression, in contrast to other penguins. They huddle close together, forming a kind of armoured shell against the cold, exposing as little as possible of their body surface to the driving storms, while the young, who are more at risk, are protected inside the shield. In one circumstance only do the birds become agitated. As soon as a chick forsakes the hatching-fold at the base of an adult penguin's belly, there is a rough-and-tumble among those penguins without a chick, who all want to adopt it. Thus the chicks have plenty of providers, not just the real parents. Eggs and young are cared for jointly by the colony, so that it maintains itself despite the cold (Portmann, *The Social Life of Animals*).

Because of the protection its members give one another, a group can resist poisons and injurious chemicals better than separate individuals. In a laboratory, goldfish in batches of ten were exposed to colloidal silver, which for them is poisonous. The same test was carried out with isolated goldfish. On average, the groups of goldfish remained alive nearly three times longer than the isolated goldfish. Small worms were exposed to ultra-violet rays. In groups, they resisted them better than when isolated. The cause has been traced to the calcium which they secrete, with which they protect one another (Allee and Bowen, *Studies in Animal Aggregations*).

Many organisms, plants as well as animals, alter an unfavourable environment in such a way as to enable others who follow them, or who are associated with them, to survive. Snails, as aquarium-keepers well know, help fish. To give an example nearer home, the degree of atmospheric pollution in our human cities depends on the plants and trees that grow in them, because vegetation produces oxygen, and trees have the capacity to absorb some of the dirty particles in the atmosphere. In the animal world there are many mutually advantageous alliances. Parasites are often deliberately tolerated by larger animals because they keep them clean.

Some vital processes are conveniently slowed down as a result of the social group, others are as conveniently speeded up. The spermatozoa of many aquatic organisms die more rapidly when disseminated than when together. Indeed, Allee sees this as an example of how competition may have co-operative results: the spermatozoa, when together as a group, compete with each other for the limited space available, and, as a result of this competition, live longer. Various sorts of protozoa increase the rate of their asexual reproduction when they are together in a sufficiently large group. Experiments with cockroaches, goldfish and members of the genus of fish *cryprinodon* have revealed that they learn more quickly in the company of their own species than they do alone. On the other hand, Ralph Fried and others have demonstrated that human young do not thrive if their socio-emotional relations are disturbed.

There is no need for me to describe in detail the perfect forms of mutual aid which ants, wasps, termites, bees, beetles and other insects have developed. The astonishment aroused by the discoveries regarding their social life, at a time when it was still generally believed that competition and mutual conflict were the 'law of nature', has made their sublime organisations sufficiently familiar. Wheeler, who in 1923 published his celebrated *Social Life Among the Insects*, is convinced that even the so-called solitary species of animals are, of necessity, more or less co-operative members of associations of animals, and that animals not only compete with one another, but also – and more especially –

co-operate, in order to ensure for themselves companions and a greater degree of security.

The attraction exerted by a school of fish, a flock of birds or a herd of mammals is in direct proportion to its size. K.A. Lorenz says that one reason why the swarm or flock offers protection to the individual is that the predator cannot concentrate on one exemplar without disregarding all the rest, so that it is continually distracted and finds it impossible to seize on one. Again, even in *Aggression in Animals and Man*, Lorenz has to stress the social attributes, in particular of the higher mammals: 'The ancestor whom we share with the chimpanzee was undoubtedly at least as loyal a companion to his friend as a wild goose or a jackdaw and certainly a baboon or a wolf.' Lonely, deserted mammals are helpless and afflicted: 'A single chimpanzee is no chimpanzee.' According to Fraser Darling, fallow deer show the same respect for their elders as do chimpanzees (Kortlandt). A group of Dutch zoologists has even observed of these animals that they grieve for their dead. That there is a tendency to more deeply-felt forms of social life the more 'highly' developed a species becomes, may perhaps be explained by pointing – as the zoologist Bourlière does (1952) – to the fact that there is in evolution a tendency to increasing independence of the material environment, and, as a result, increasing dependence on the social environment. Or, *vice versa*, might it not be that a more intense social life results in an increasing independence of the environment?

Higher animals remain longer in the nest, and this affords a stimulus to social life. Quite often the females are not in a position to provide their young with food; the males then go on long hunting expeditions to procure it for them. Wolves carry pieces of meat in their mouths for their females and their offspring over as long a distance as twenty-five kilometers. The African hyena, on arriving home after a long expedition, vomits up his food so that his family can eat it. These predators are even popularly credited with possessing a communal stomach. Knowing all this, it is hard, surely, to interpret *homo homini lupus* as anything but a compliment. Most of this was unknown to biologists in Kropotkin's day and they derided his theories without being able to refute them. Today, the social aspects of animal life are a focal point of interest. As Portmann says: 'We recognise that the life of all the higher animals is social from the very start, that social behaviour in its most diverse aspects is an essential feature of the higher animals . . . Innumerable touches of feeling, postures, gestures, noises, signs, contacts, on a superficial view meaningless and previously ignored, have suddenly taken on a meaning; and this increased interest has assigned to a lot of inconspicuous or hidden structures a role in social existence. Expressions of higher life, long unappreciated, now stand fully illuminated on a big new biological platform.'

Psychologists are discovering that an element indispensable for social life, altruism – in which not even Freud had shown the slightest interest – is intrinsic to the motivation of men and animals. In Hebb's behaviouristic terms this means that it is not dependent on primary or secondary reinforcements. The knowledge that you have helped someone else yields enough satisfaction. Hebb distinguishes between co-operative behaviour and altruism. Altruism presupposes ideas, co-operation does not. Since he attributes consciousness to apes but not to ants, only the former, according to Hebb, are altruistic in their conduct. The examples he gives are that apes efficiently provide food for other apes in distress and that dolphins will steer a companion who is short of oxygen to the ocean surface (Hebb, *A Textbook of Psychology*).

Kropotkin bases his view of morality on his discovery of the mutual aid practised by men and animals as a means of preserving the species. Morals are a product of group solidarity and can be simply expressed in the ancient maxim: 'Do unto others as you wish them to do unto you'. Kant's account of the origin and effectiveness of this categorical imperative is, in Kropotkin's view, insufficient. As Kropotkin says in *Ethics*, after four years of deep reflection Kant in effect admitted that he could not solve the problem; for in his *Philosophical Theory of Religion* he adduced man's divine origin as the explanation; and to Kropotkin, the materialist, that amounted to failure. Kropotkin looked for a scientific explanation of the moral instinct in man.

In support of his opinion that such an explanation must lie

in the struggle to ensure the survival of the species through mutual aid, he cites, besides Bakunin, the 'other' Darwin. Darwin, in the *Descent of Man*, saw the authentic basis of all moral feelings 'in the social instinct that induces the animal to take pleasure in the companionship of his kind, to feel some measure of sympathy for them and to perform various services on their behalf'. Although the social instinct is acquired by man in his state of origin, it is the motive power for our best actions.

Co-operation and sympathy, according to Kropotkin, are a constituional need of every living creature. If by helping someone you have to forgo this or that pleasure, this should not be regarded as in any way a conquest of self. 'They tell us, for instance', he says in *Ethics*, 'that there is no greater virtue, no greater triumph of the spiritual over the physical, than self-sacrifice for the well-being of our fellow men. But it is a fact that self-sacrifice in the interest of a nest of ants, or for the safety of a flock of birds, a herd of antelopes or a troupe of monkeys *is a zoological fact of daily occurrence in nature*!' The happiness of each individual is intimately bound up with the happiness of all. You always act well, says the author of *The Anarchist Morality*, if you seek the happiness of all. Is it your own happiness you seek? If you limit yourself to that, you will not find it. You will find it, more or less fortuitously, in pursuing the happiness of the community. Someone who does that, and in so doing 'sacrifices' something, cannot be called either an altruist or an egoist. The opposition is a false one. Egoism and altruism are one and the same; if they were in absolute opposition, evolution would have been impossible. The man who lives satisfied and happy amid the wretchedness of others, and has become rich by exploiting his fellow men, builds his house on sand. He does not understand that the aim of every individual is to lead an intensive life and that the greatest intensity is found in the deepest solidarity, in the identity of the individual with all around him. The happiness of the individual and his group are indissolubly linked. Because the contrast between egoism and altruism is absurd (though Hebb still makes the mistake of setting them against each other), Kropotkin also opposes the utilitarians such as Bentham and

James and John Stuart Mill, who searched for a compromise between them. Furthermore, Kropotkin could not, like them, effect a compromise with oppression and exploitation.

When the spiritual and mental capacities of a species are highly developed, as is the case with human beings, the social instinct is bound to evolve further still. In men the principle of justice and equality advances above and beyond itself to become morality. 'Morality' is interpreted by Kropotkin in a narrow sense as readiness deliberately to sacrifice oneself, to eschew revenge, to give more than one has obtained. 'Without equality there is no justice, and without justice there is no morality.' If society recognised only equality, says Kropotkin, if everyone were an honest trader, and had pledged himself with painful meticulousness to give to others no more than he received from them, society would die.

To make clear that people are more inclined to give than receive, Kropotkin based himself on the theory of a French philosopher, Guyau (1854-1888), whom he much admired. Guyau thought that because the 'life energy' was so abundant, it was always trying to find an outlet, and nothing could restrain it. This was why we are inclined always to give more then we receive. 'Life can only maintain itself by manifesting itself.'

Kropotkin reproves the utilitarians, with their theory that 'the good' is whatever yields a maximum of enjoyment and a minimum of pain and difficulty, and that in this way you can make a calculation of good and bad – a petty view indeed! To be able to act is to be obliged to do so. 'A plant cannot desist from flowering; although sometimes this means that it will die. Yet flower it must – the sap continues to rise,' says Kropotkin, in *The Anarchist Morality*, quoting Guyau. It is the same with man. 'He stores energy. He must express himself. He gives without counting the cost; without that he cannot live. And if he has to die, it makes no difference. If it is there, the sap rises. *Be strong.* Abound with energy, in passionate feeling and in strength of mind and spirit, and you will pour your intelligence, your affection, your power of action upon other people.'

Kropotkin sees in human history a persistent attempt to interpret the fundamental idea of mutual aid on a broader basis. At first it encompasses only the clan; then the tribe, then a federation of tribes; then whole nations; and in the modern period it is proposed as an ideal for the whole of mankind. Moreover, it has gradually been refined. In primitive Buddhism, in Stoicism and early Christianity, in the writings of certain Muslim teachers, in the early Reformation and above all in the ethical and philosophical trend of the nineteenth and twentieth centuries, Kropotkin sees the notion of revenge progressively rejected. 'Loftier principles, namely, no revenge for injury suffered, and freely giving more than one could hope to receive from one's neighbour in return, are declared to be the true foundation of morality – above equality, above equity or right or justice – because they are better guides to happiness.' The apotheosis of Kropotkin's morality is the happiness deriving from the solidarity of an integrated human race: 'It is not man's vocation to direct his actions toward a love that is personal or at most embraces the tribe, but toward the consciousness of his unity with every other human being' (*Mutual Aid*).

Kropotkin's conception of morality is quite different from the Marxists'. They say that morality is relative, and always depends on the class in power. But to Kropotkin morality is absolute, implicit in nature, and perfected so that evolution advances and living organisms are refined. Kropotkin interprets morality in an evolutionary, the Marxists in a revolutionary, context. In fact, in the Marxist conception of evolution we find Darwinism: there is a ceaseless struggle between classes and the moralities appropriate to each, the 'fittest' of which prevails in any given period. In the industrial age the proletariat must win because it is the 'fittest class'. Kropotkin, too, thinks that the proletariat will – when co-operation and reasonableness ultimately get the upper hand; but after its victory, the day after the revolution, the proletariat ceases to be a proletariat, because then a beginning is made with the total co-operation of all people. Kropotkin did not contemplate a class dictatorship.

I think that Kropotkin was too optimistic concerning the period after the revolution, in which it will be necessary for a time to suppress the former ruling class, though you can see this, as Kropotkin did, as setting them free; for it is not a question just of liberating the proletariat, but of liberating all of us from antiquated structures and thought-patterns which are bound to disappear. Yet I believe he was right to envisage morality as evolutionary and absolute, that is, as independent of any particular class. To underline that point I would like to compare his conception of morality with Trotsky's, who set out the Marxist interpretation very clearly in his short book, *Their Morality and Ours*.

Trotsky says that morality is nothing more than a weapon in the armoury of the class struggle. The different moralities of the ruling and oppressed classes have no absolute significance, but are only a means of deploying the power of one class or the other. There is nothing unalterable about morality. A morality standing over and above class is out of the question. Morality arises only in an antagonistic environment.

Kropotkin, on the other hand, says that morality has always existed, both in nature and among the human beings who form part of it. A morality of mutual aid is found among plants, animals *and* men. He illustrates this in, for instance, *The Anarchist Morality*: 'Forel, the great expert on ants, has shown with the help of a mass of factual observations that if an ant has filled itself with honey, and meets other ants with empty stomachs, they immediately ask it for something to eat. It is an obligation among these tiny insects for the fully-fed ant to disgorge some honey, so that its hungry friends may be satisfied in their turn. Well now, ask the ants whether it is all right to deny food to ants from the same colony, after one has had one's own share. With no uncertain actions they will answer you that it is very bad. Such an egoistic ant would be dealt with more harshly than enemies of a different species.'

According to Kropotkin, therefore, morality is not something that has arisen in an antagonistic environment; for it prevails as much in classless nature as among primitive tribal peoples who are still strangers to class antagonisms. 'Proletarian' or 'bourgeois' morality rests ultimately on the same basis, the social instinct, the need to attune behaviour to the preservation of the species. Whatever class or party we belong to, we are all first and foremost human beings. We could say, in support of Kropotkin, that morality is universal and absolute because it has arisen among all species in parallel ways, as an adaptation to the given fact of the group and of the difficult circumstances with which nature confronts us. In all species, corresponding rules of conduct have emerged, designed to make existence possible. Kropotkin believed that this universal morality was disrupted at a particular moment in human history by the appearance of a group of usurpers of power, 'the sorcerers, rain-makers, miracle-workers, priests, leaders of warlike hordes' and so on, from whom came the ruling classes, who with their coercive methods disrupted the morality of voluntary mutual aid. The people must bring them down, if the universal morality of nature is to flourish among men. So while Trotsky considers the subjugation of nature to be a goal of socialism, Kropotkin sees it as a goal of the socialist society to live in harmony with the (moral) laws of nature. Trotsky wants to lord it over nature, Kropotkin to listen to nature.

While Trotsky looks upon morality as an instrument in the class struggle, Kropotkin concludes that the oppressed class is the instrument whereby natural morality will independently re-establish its rights. In the final analysis, Kropotkin's morality is classless, while Trotsky's is indissolubly tied to the proletariat, whether subjugated or dominant. Kropotkin's morality is aimed, in the end, at the abolition of power, Trotsky's at establishing it. 'To reap wheat you must sow wheat', says Trotsky. He is arguing that the means must accord with the end – which is the liberation of mankind. It is the worthiest notion in his book; but it clashes with other ideas of his to which he gives more emphasis. He recommends a jesuitical form of organization as the best possible means of overthrowing the ruling class and heralding the day of liberation. He believes that opposing armies should be symmetrical, and that the underdog must adopt the methods and organization of the oppressor. Trotsky was a Commander-in-chief of the Red Army, and his way of thinking is characterised by the frequent use of military metaphors. His thinking is consistently Marxist; the antithesis is a product of the thesis: 'The abolition of self-alienation proceeds in the same way as self-alienation'. Thus the antithesis takes over certain crucial hallmarks of the thesis itself.

Trotsky wanted the impossible. You cannot imitate the enemy's methods without taking over his goals. Trotsky says himself: 'The man who knuckles under to the rules prescribed by his opponent will never get the better of him!' For this reason, the Bolsheviks' success was more apparent than real. They submitted to Tsarist requirements in administration (Lenin's hierarchical military organization) and methods of combat (full-scale war, torture and the taking of hostages). The inevitable result, in broad outline, was that the Bolsheviks maintained intact the model of Tsarist domination, and even breathed new life into it. Imperialism, class dictatorship and censorship characterise the communist state in Russia today no less than they did its Tsarist predecessor. The similarity extends to the very details of Tsarist techniques of repression: political opponents are declared insane and incarcerated in lunatic asylums. Stalinist Russia was not merely a reaction from the 1917 revolution (as Trotsky, to comfort himself, asserted); it was the logical outcome of these aspects of Bolshevism.

Trotsky argued that the analogy between Stalinism and Fascism, which even he recognised, is a purely formal one. They serve completely opposite classes and therefore opposite ends. Once more, it is clear that the substantial content of a class is not the decisive factor for morality; for anyone who avails himself of the forms of Fascism is sowing the seeds of Fascism. In the form, the seed, is already enclosed the full-grown plant. The plant is a carnivorous one; and the crop ought not to surprise us.

Kropotkin's interpretation of the history of morality is optimistic. For the time being, the extension of the principle of mutual aid to include the population of the entire world is still overshadowed by the resentment which governments and peoples (the latter seduced by the former) bear toward one another. But Kropotkin's vision can act as an ideal or sign-post for the men and women of today and of the future. Our only chance of saving the human race is to base our morality on the social instinct for preserving the species that finds its foremost expression in mutual aid. With that in view, Kropotkin's morality is not too optimistic.

Kropotkin's morality is, above all, human. By stressing that the morality of rulers and rebels alike ultimately rests on the same social instinct (even if it is usually interpreted too narrowly and is confined to too small a group), he avoids the Marxists' discriminatory view of morality, from which there can only emerge new types of oppression – of different groups this time. The revolution must avoid not only exchanging one authority for another, but also removing one form of oppression in favour of another. Kropotkin would have freedom, whole and indivisible, for everyone.

Kropotkin interprets morality in an evolutionary context; but at the same time he insists on revolution. For him, revolutions are part of an all-embracing evolution. When the river of life is temporarily obstructed by obstacles like dictatorship or oppression, then a revolutionary breakthrough is necessary. But his concern is with the river, not with the breakthrough as such. The future is already enclosed within the present; the future is not the antithesis of the here and now. Kropotkin's insight teaches us that we have to find ways which do not, like Trotsky's, bear within them the germ of a new tyranny.

Kropotkin was excessively optimistic in his estimate of the reasonableness of human beings. He held, unrealistically, that you should be able to break the resistance of capitalists, and authorities generally, by presenting them with rational arguments. In that respect, he was one of the last products of the Enlightenment, in the rationalistic tradition which had begun in France at the time of the great Revolution. Authority is not, as Kropotkin thought, just a question of superstition, of 'magicians, rain-makers, miracle-workers' and so forth; it is not simply imposed upon us, but has its source inside ourselves – in our baseless fear of living our own lives, and of steering society ourselves instead of having it run for us. Our anti-authoritarian revolution is more difficult than any revolution has been in the past. Besides the socio-economic structure of society, we have to change also our own psychological structure. The screwed-up little dictator in each of us will have to abandon his entrenched position. It has to be recognised that anti-authoritarian upbringing and education, in which Kropotkin had such faith as revolutionary methods, are proving effective. From the least authoritarian schools there come the most revolutionary youngsters. Democracy at school and university is something that escalates. The more quickly democratic education is implemented right down the line, and the sooner project-based education is introduced, the shorter will be the road to the total, anti-authoritarian revolution. But apart from that, such irrational emotions as anxiety and lust for power will have to be countered with the irrational emotions of love and solidarity. The eroticising of .society, which is now in process as the restrictive division of roles between man and women disappears, is helping to dissolve our need for authority. But the process is threatened: it can be a real contribution only if it is not controlled from above or totally commercialised. Our anti-authoritarian revolution will require more time and more radical activity than any previous revolution. It is a revolutionary evolution of man and society, of mind and matter as a single entity.

CHAPTER THREE

The Peacock-Butterfly: or Co-operation and Aggression, an alternating current

So far we have been dealing with facts and ideas that give grounds for hope. But if Kropotkin had failed to recognise that in nature there is aggression as well as co-operation, he would have been a foolish gnome indeed.

Kropotkin did not deny the existence of aggression as a factor in evolution; but in confronting his contemporaries, whose Darwinian view of society prevented them from seeing beyond it, he felt that it was essential, from a polemical point of view, to put the emphasis on co-operative behaviour. In the Preface to *Mutual Aid* he says of his book: 'It is about the law of mutual aid, viewed as one of the chief factors in evolution – not in any sense about *all* the factors in evolution and their interactive value; and this first book had to be written before the second became possible.' Kropotkin never produced a book on the mutual relationship between co-operation and aggression. He was too preoccupied with demonstrating that there is co-operation in nature – an idea which only his political friends were prepared to accept. But now that the importance of Kropotkin's ideas is admitted even in 'official scientific circles', thanks to the work of biologists like Wheeler, Allee, Montagu, Schneirla, Portmann, Tinbergen and others, the time has come to investigate the difficult but revealing relationship that in fact exists between aggression and co-operation. Although these two forces are antagonistic – in the form of competitiveness, aggression certainly seems to be diametrically opposed to co-operation – they are in fact the two main factors in evolution.

Aggresion is an alternative strategy to which the species may have recourse, for self-preservation, when co-operation proves inadequate. Aggression expresses the force of repulsion that can exist between individuals. Often, when two aggressive members of a species confront and repel each other, they delimit their territory. According to Konrad Lorenz, in *Aggression in Animals and Men*, it is an observed fact that feline animals mark off their territory so sharply by their aggressive behaviour that Intruder *A* will invariable be worsted on the home ground of *B*, because, morally, *A*'s position there is so much weaker. *B* will pursue *A* all the way to *A*'s own territory, where *A* will suddenly turn and chase back *B*, who is now the weaker party because he is on strange territory. This chasing to and fro will be repeated several times until both come to a halt, in a menacing confrontation, but no longer attacking each other. At that moment their strength, morally speaking, is equally matched, because they are exactly on the boundary between their territories. The territories are marked out by the diffusion of signals such as scents (urine, in the case of dogs) or sounds (as in birds) or colours (fish). Territories occur among insects, lobsters, fish, birds and mammals. The function of such territories is ecological. In order to prevent exhaustion of the soil, or of vegetation, or of animal life, some special arrangement is needed. An equable distribution of the members of a species, accomplished by aggression, is just as necessary as the similar division in our society among specialists – doctors, grocers, shoemakers, milkmen.

Might not the same function have been served equally well by co-operation? My impression is no. Co-operation is first and foremost a power of attraction, and is therefore not suitable for engendering the effect of repulsion between animals even though the repulsion takes place in as equable a manner as possible. Insofar as aggression can be avoided, it is avoided. But when the signals are being ignored, a display of aggressive emotion is essential to ensure that they are effective, just as some affectionate feeling must of necessity be shown in order to maintain co-operation. Love and aggression sanction, respectively, co-operation and competition.

The display of aggressive emotion hardly ever leads to serious trouble. Fighting, particularly among the higher animals, is ritualised. The biological purpose of aggression is to subjugate or ward off an antagonist, not to kill him. The loser can let it be known by certain gestures that he admits defeat. He can cringe, for instance – the opposite of erecting the hairs – conceal his natural armament, invitingly present his weakest spot (e.g. the neck to his conqueror, or, irrespective of the opponent's sex, assume a copulation-posture. Chimpanzees, as a sign of surrender, extend the hand. The heavier the armament of the animals in question, the more surely do the 'breaking mechanisms' of their placatory and submissive gestures operate. It would not be in the interest of the species for one of the two to die.

These repellent functions are always discharged in the way that will most favour the preservation of the species. Concerning such breaking mechanisms. Lorenz says in his *Aggresion in Animals and Men*: 'Physiological mechanisms compel animals to adopt a disinterested kind of behaviour which is consonant with the well-being of the community, just as in us human beings it is commanded by a moral law within us.' In animals, even the mechanism of aggression invariably has a constructive purpose. Would it be going too far to call 'territorial aggression' a pseudo-co-operative type of behaviour? After all, the display of aggressive and repulsive emotions does achieve something (namely, diffusion) which is in the interest of both parties.

Other functions fulfilled by aggression are the building up of a hierarchy and the protection of the young of the species. Why do most higher animals have a hierarchical social structure? I would not claim to be able to give a precise answer; but I can see what the advantages are. The males at the top of the hierarchy acquire the most females. This is in the interest of the species, because it would not be good if the weakest and least suitable parents were to have the most offspring. Again, it is in the interest of the species that the weaker individuals should be protected by the hierarchy. The lower their fellows are in the scale, the more sympathy the top males feel for them. The inferior males are not in competition with the top male; in a sense he is dependent on them, because if those lower down were to disappear from the hierarchy, he would lose his prestige. At the same time, the inferior and weaker males derive benefit from the superior ones. When certain groups of animals come under attack, they form a circle, with the strongest on the perimeter and the weakest safe inside the circle. The whole group can profit from the experience and cleverness of their leader. S.L. Washburne and Irven de Vore (quoted by Lorenz) have observed how a troupe of baboons in open country were saved from a lion by their organised response to the perceptiveness of their aged leader. Unnoticed by the lion, the leader was able to watch its position and, giving it a wide berth, cautiously lead the other apes to safety in the trees. No ape other than the leader would have been able to do this, because they would not imitate anyone else. Only the old and wise will be imitated, for it is only they who are worth imitating.

The hierarchy is an individualising factor. It differentiates individuals by their roles. On the other hand, a hierarchy is the organically structured product of a group of individuals possessing a range of inherited aptitudes, experience and attributes (such as territories). An elementary hierarchy is likewise indispensable for a group of human beings; a flexible hierarchy gives a group elasticity.

The aggression associated with hierarchy almost never claims any victims. Crane, who has studied the duelling practised by signal-crabs, says of it: 'What most observers had noticed was here confirmed: namely, that only very rarely do woundings occur, even though it may come to a duel with the claws of each fastened on the other. I have myself seen but one instance of mutilation and that of the top of a pincer' (J. Crane, *Crabs of the Genus Uca from the West Coast of Central America*).

The repellent effect of aggression makes it possible for a hierarchy to emerge. The power of attraction that co-operation implies cannot have this effect; for, far from distributing individuals on various social levels, it draws them together on to a single level. Obviously, the hierarchy formed by aggression, with its individualising distribution of tasks and its efficient organisation, ultimately serves a co-operative purpose.

Most adult animals adopt a protective attitude towards the young, especially if they are members of the same species; human beings also do this. But there are predators belonging to other species who may prove a danger to the young. Therefore, for as long as she has to look after her brood, the mother is armed with extra powers of aggression, to prevent such enemies from approaching the nest. Could this be replaced by direct co-operation? That would be feasible only if the mother were endowed with an ability to distinguish between animals dangerous to her young and those who are not. Since most animals do not have this capacity, except in some cases in which the mother can distinguish the father, their aggression is directed against everything that moves around the nest. The existence of aggressive predators brings me to that function of aggression which is most difficult to understand: hunting.

Why has evolution produced hunting predators? Even this activity, the hardest form of aggression to accept, includes pseudo-co-operative tendencies. The difference between hunting and aggression between members of the same species is that in hunting there are individual victims. Their death has to be seen in the light of eternity, in the consoling realisation that they do not die in vain, and that in the end no form of energy is transient.

Species are never exterminated *in toto* by another species which treats them as quarry; for the prey always develop counter-weapons. This is the pseudo-co-operative tendency: through conflict, both hunter and hunted refine their organisms. 'The speed of hoofed animals' says Lorenz, 'fosters in the feline predators who hunt them tremendous ability to leap and sharp-nailed claws, whilst they on the other hand help to develop in the prey finer and finer senses and a faster gait. Apart from that, the counter-attack mounted by many animals who are preyed upon once again demonstrates the value of co-operation. All types of geese know that if they charge at a wolf, hissing and in close formation, they can so harass him that he will run away. In the same way, herds of zebras in formation will even drive off leopards. The fact that they co-operate gives a decisive strength to their aggression. Yet aggression is never an end in itself. It is an alternative strategy which achieves what direct co-operation cannot. From this I am bound to conclude that *there is a special reciprocal relationship between aggression and co-operation.*

This relationship is a dual one. On the one hand, it is a higher form of mutual aid. Aggression fulfils the repellent functions which co-operation, because it attracts, cannot fulfil; and co-operation, through its capacity for organisation, can provide aggression with a special kind of strength which unadulterated aggression alone, because it repels, is unable to acquire. Aggressiveness induces animals to delimit territories so as to serve a higher co-operative end, namely, the purposive exploitation of the terrain by the species. The urge to co-operate induces zebras to form intimidating groups; and it is this that makes their aggression toward the leopard so effective. The aggressive driving away of elements dangerous to the brood by the parents, or by the mother alone, is a function that could be achieved through co-operation only if there were no such thing as hunting – which, as we have seen, itself serves a pseudo-co-operative goal (the refining of the senses and the organism). The co-operative behaviour which has its most demonstrative expression in sexual intercourse between two animals is a function that cannot possibly be taken over by the alternative strategy, aggression, precisely because the latter is repulsive, and not attractive, in its effect. Similarly, in the creation of a hierarchy, aggressive behaviour between rivals cannot be replaced by co-operation, because co-operation is characterised by the power of attraction. The way in which, once it has arisen, a hierarchy co-operates and give tranquility to the group, cannot be replaced by an aggressive method. No protection we give to animals can ever be a substitute for the function of predators in hunting their prey, stimulating as it does the process of refining organisms. But the result of the co-operation between ox-pecker and rhinoceros (the ox-pecker prevents the rhinoceros's parasites from becoming too numerous) and the result of animal-protection on man's part, cannot possibly be attained by aggression. Hunting is the counterpart and complement to a self-sacrificing love. All this reveals the relationship of mutual aid which exists between aggression and co-operation, the two main factors in evolution, and links them together in a positive fashion. It is a pity that Kropotkin never carried his idea of mutual aid beyond its application to individuals and groups. It is equally operative as a relation between these two apparently opposite principles of evolution. That Kropotkin never got that far is partly due to the state of science at the time. The constructive power of many forms of aggression had not yet been recognised. People took it to be a purely destructive force, as many still do today.

On the other hand, there is a negative relationship between aggression and co-operation: a higher form of repulsion. Aggression and co-operation shun each other. When two parties are in conflict, the existing co-operation between them will wane or even cease altogether, while in contrast, the internal co-operation will intensify at the same rate as the aggression between the contending parties. Jesus of Nazareth was crucified by his enemies, who were filled with aggression and fear, while he preached love and co-operation. Thomas Huxley, author of the *Struggle for Life Manifesto* and champion of aggression, was so repelled by Kropotkin's call for co-operation that, as we have seen, he was one of the few scientists of note who refused to sign the petition for his release.

On the one hand, then, there is a positive relationship between aggression and co-operation, which through the mutually complementary character of these two poles has a higher co-operative function; on the other hand there is a negative relationship which, through their mutually repellent character, has a higher repulsive and actually destructive function. This dual relationship is the *alternating current* linking co-operation and aggression with each other. That alternating process explains why love can sometimes turn to hate, while former enemies may become good friends. The higher co-operative function of the positive relationship between aggression and co-operation tends towards life, which it makes possible. The higher repellent function of the negative relationship between aggression and co-operation tends towards death, which it can occasion. It is a destructive force.

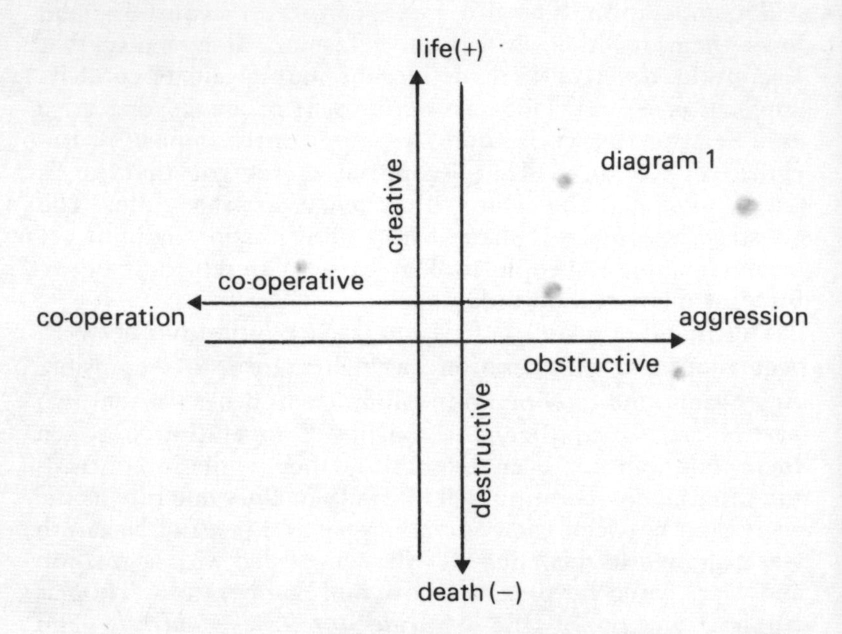

Co-operation and aggression, linked by an alternating current of attraction and repulsion, together form one axis of a system of co-ordinates. The other axis, perpendicular to it, is constituted by the higher co-operative and repulsive functions, being creative and destructive forces which are ultimately linked together by the poles of life and death. The two axes stand together in a mysterious mutual relationship: and they form the tensional field that we are accustomed to call life. At the intersection of this system of co-ordinates is the individual, the individual event, the species or any unit on which we choose to concentrate our attention. Aggression and co-operation are dynamos powered by the same force: the 'current' alternating between attraction and repulsion. Obviously, therefore, a relationship that starts by being aggressive can later become co-operative and friendly. At any rate, I certainly have experiences of this kind, and a lot of other people must have them as well. Lorenz actually believes that all positive personal ties arise out of aggressiveness. He illustrates this with another example from the animal kingdom. A female has young, and so is aggressive towards everything that moves in the vicinity of the nest. However, in order to look after her young she needs the help of a male; so that towards *him* she must not be aggressive. How does nature solve this problem? The female of the pair learns to distinguish the male in question from his performance of a particular ceremonial. This engenders a positive 'affection'. Lorenz's thesis that all love is a product of aggressiveness goes too far. It suffers from the same one-sidedness as the thesis that everything is the result of co-operation (an error which Kropotkin did not commit). Lorenz's thesis resembles all too closely the Fascist notion that war is the mother of all things. Understandably enough, therefore, Lorenz is on the Right, politically speaking. His attempt to show that aggression is often constructive may be regarded as highly successful; but his conclusion is unconvincing and illogical. Co-operation and cohesion, as Kropotkin and other like-minded people have pointed out, are indispensable to the emergence of life. I cannot see why spontaneous affection should have to emerge in a roundabout way *via* aggression, as Lorenz insists, rather than from the power of attraction which positive and negative particles, unicellular creatures, plants, insects, animals and men all exercise on one another. If aggression were the fundamental emotional drive in nature, the destructive forces in nature would play such a dominant role that evolution of any kind would be out of the question.

Positive and negative particles do not simply attract one another; to a certain extent they repel one another too. In other words, aggression and co-operation are two poles of the same vital force: they arise at one and the same moment.

In the 'Provo' period, I knew nothing of the optimism that comes from realising that all things are linked together in solidarity and exhibit an active principle of mutual aid. My protest arose out of despair. As I said in *Provo no. 1.*, 'We are struck by the ultimate meaninglessness of our actions, we fully believe that neither Johnson nor Kosygin is going to listen to us . . .' 'Provo' did not sufficiently realise that all this mental outlook was coloured by the gloomy philosophical tradition in science that started with Malthus, was carried on by Darwin and up to a point by the Marxists, and in the twentieth century has produced psycho-analysis and existentialism. The bearers of this tradition have always regarded 'the struggle for existence' as a competitive battle (even if, as the Marxists thought, it was being waged not by individuals but by classes). For all of them, conflict, aggressiveness, is the central force. They all offer the same remedies for the aggression which constitutes a chronic threat to society: authority. Authority has to be powerful, in order to crush the danger represented by the original sin of aggressiveness in man. As a result, these authoritarian thinkers have usually also been pessimists; they had regarded authority as necessary, and yet as bad. That Marx and the Marxists form an exception to this pessimism does not speak altogether in their favour; they were all too ready to speak of authority in optimist terms.

After the First World War, Kropotkin was forgotten. Apart from a tiny anarchist group, few remained interested in the theoretical expostion of mutual aid. The moral catastrophe of the war and the victories of Fascism and Stalinism once more fixed attention exclusively on the 'aggression' school of thinking, whose theories met with more approval in journalistic circles.

The most important of modern conflict-thinkers was Sigmund Freud, an anti-Kropotkinian in every respect. Freud said of himself that he could find within him no trace of any feeling of solidarity with the universe. The 'oceanic sense' that forms the basis of religious thought he explained in a somewhat denigratory vein, in *Civilisation and its Discontents*, in terms of the infantile helplessness which struggles for a union of the 'I' with the outer world. It is a residue of early childhood, which in older people often disappears. He sees the need for solidarity with a universal 'all' as first and foremost a lack of emancipation, a quest for comfort and consolation. To the religious mentality, in the literal sense of a feeling of relatedness and solidarity, Freud can assign no value, because he cannot reconcile it with his individualist and egoistic view of man.

Freud does not reckon with the possibility that society

may be based on the social character of human beings. To Freud, people are kept together by the necessity of working, and by sexual love – *the* example of human happiness. For him, universal love is no more than an inferior, frustrated distortion of sexual love. In fact universal love is only possible in the case of a very eccentric person, because human beings in general are not worth the trouble of loving.

Freud takes a step back in the direction of utilitarianism. Whereas Kropotkin and Guyay had said that man has a surplus of love, or of affection and energy, which he must pour out in abundance, Freud says, 'Be sparing with love, realize that it is something precious which you cannot give away just like that'. With Freud, utilitarianism turns into a psychological commercialism. 'If I cherish someone else, in one way or another he has to deserve it.' I must be able to use the other person as an ideal, or I must be able to identify myself with him so that I can love myself in him. Only in those instances does the other person *deserve* my love; a free consumption of love does not come into it. Nor, according to Freud, should you spontaneously expend energy. 'Just as the discreet man of business will avoid tying up his entire capital in one place, so worldly wisdom may counsel us not to expect a single endeavour to yield total satisfaction.' It is true, of course, he said, that you should not live like a monomaniac; yet his example of the businessman more or less reduces living to a matter of cheese-paring calculation, a profitable industrial enterprise, a frustrating refusal to throw yourself enthusiastically into anything. All the same, the state of infantile dependence at the beginning of life is preferable to what comes later, if we are to believe Freud himself. Of course, it was not much fun in the first place to be tossed into the world with a mortal shock; for the initial *Angst*, which we have to carry about with us for the rest of our lives, originated at the moment of separation from the mother (*Inhibitions, Symptoms and Anxiety*). But after this fearsome event (contemporary psychology has fortunately dropped this interpretation of birth) the growing child must face the prospect of a number of distressing psychic processes, the chief of which is the Oedipus complex (the need to kill one's father in order to monopolise the mother's love). The socialisation of the young as individuals can be brought about only with the greatest difficulty. Freud's disciple Mitscherlich also sees 'empathizing' as a slow and painful business.

The adult individual has to engage in an unending struggle with the community. The 'I', egged on by the gratification-principle, has certain main interests which clash with those of the community as a whole. The urge of a human being to be free is in conflict with the culture, which imposes every possible restriction on the individual, while the individual can expect from such restrictions nothing but neurosis. Individual freedom is never a consequence of culture. The freedom of the individual, according to Freud, was at its greatest before the beginning of every culture. Freud seems to have forgotten that man's culture is his nature, and that without culture and without other human beings he is not viable at all.

In the last analysis, Freud's pessimistic view of culture reduces itself to Hobbes' old-fashioned notion of general war – the war of all against all. He echoes Hobbes almost to the letter when, in *Civilization and its Discontents*, he says that the tendency, inherent in culture, to bring people into unity 'is opposed by their strong natural feelings of aggression, the hostility felt by each for all and by all for each'. Thus creation scarcely gives people the opportunity to become happy. There are at least three sources of wretchedness: the external world all about us, our body (destined to decay) and our dealings with our fellow men. A little happiness may be found, merely as an 'episodic phenomenon', by way of contrast to the normal unhappiness that inevitably dominates our life. Marcuse, in *Eros and Civilization*, rightly calls attention to the fact that, of the three sources of affliction mentioned by Freud, at least two are historical and therefore alterable in character: our relationship to nature and the form of human society.

The saying *homo homini lupus* reappears in Freud's thought. Man is actuated by the blind passions of the subconscious Id, in which the dominant factor is the death-wish. 'The goal of all life is death' is his sombre message in *Beyond the Pleasure Principle*. Freud envisages aggression as an element of the death-impulse. His work presents our aggressiveness as, in the first place, a destructive passion. After one has read Lorenz's *On Aggression in Animals and Men*, where the constructive results of various kinds of aggression in nature are convincingly demonstrated, Freud's presentation of aggressiveness strikes one as sterile and obsolete. According to Lorenz, man is bent on exploiting, violating, despoiling, humiliating, torturing and killing his fellows. How can culture, which is constantly threatened by our over-ruling need for aggression and destruction, maintain itself, except by means of stern repression? Like Hobbes, Freud believed that subjugation of the individual is inevitable, because the free individual constitutes a danger to society. Freud did not state this conclusion as explicitly as I am stating it here; but it is the inescapable consequence of his theory of culture. In *The Future of an Illusion* he admits: 'Every culture has to be built on coercion and the denial of instinct; it would even seem to be doubtful whether, without being coerced, the majority of human individuals would be prepared to submit to the toil that is necessary for earning new commodities': as though working cannot be just as well a pleasure as a plague, as though living together in community cannot provide intense satisfaction of social needs! Freud was able to see only the repressive character of society, and the ever-increasing necessity to deny the individual. Even sublimation helps only in the case of a handful of super-talented people; and even for them, sublimation does not yield the full satisfaction that comes from the unrestrained fulfilment of our untamed need for aggression. While Kropotkin maintained that freedom and the satisfaction of impulse are the very things that create culture, Freud held that it can only be created by coercion and *'Triebverzicht'* – the renunciation of instinct and of the satisfaction of impulse. Every culture must compel its members to *'Triebversagung'*, the progressive renunciation of elementary, impulsive feelings; yet because this denial of instinct always tends to self-destruction, the inescapable fate of every culture is also self-destruction. Sexuality also, says Freud, is being progressively repressed. Yet the sexual revolution, even within the framework of capitalist society, is busily disproving this theory, not just in principle but in practice. If we can succeed in rescuing sexuality from the grip of Victorian morality, and also from the grip of commercialism, then at least one aspect of repression will have disappeared. However, I do not think this is wholly possible in a capitalist society, since freedom is indivisible; it will have to be a constituent part of a total revolution. Broadly speaking, there seems to be increasing provision for us to gratify freely our need for the creative employment of leisure. And how much better and more intense could life be for the leisured population of tomorrow, if it were liberated from a society based on war, hunger, exploitation and deceit?

Freud took his conflict-thinking so far as to regard the real nature of life as intolerable for the individual. We have to fight reality at every moment. What we can do, with some chance of success, is to retreat into hermit-like solitude, cutting ourselves off completely from society; we can escape its miseries by flight into the stupors of religion or neurosis. In this context, Freud gave such rein to his pessimism that he even spoke with approval of drugs and narcotics. Finally, in 'the struggle for happiness' (the phrase reminds one strongly of Darwin), people can try to change the actual state of affairs through science and technology. But anyone who thinks that this, at last, sounds like a hopeful way out, is doomed to disappointment. For this endeavour, too, is without prospect of success. Man's psychic constitution is so highly susceptible to unhappiness that reality is always bound to be exasperating. Social reforms? We can abolish private ownership; but though there may be something to be said for that, it too leads to nothing, because human aggression simply uses the issue of proprietorial relations as an excuse for moving into action. As an instance of this, he points to Russia, where private property has not been abolished at all. The means of production there is controlled by a small bureaucracy. It does not own it officially – but what is possession other than control? Only the right of inheritance is absent. Moreover, there is such a big difference between salaries that only a vague, theoretical connection with the idea of abolishing private property remains. But Freud ignores these arguments – which were being advanced by Kropotkin and others of the same mind long before

Civilisation and its Discontents was written (1930) – and concludes despairingly: 'Maybe we should get used to the idea that there are difficulties inherent in the essential nature of culture which are not going to yield to any attempt at reform.'

One can understand why, during the Thirties, Freud the Jew did not take an optimistic view of mankind's destiny. One is even filled with admiration that he should have developed the techniques of psycho-analysis into yet another instrument for attaining insight and understanding. But we should not forget that Freud's philosophy is a rationalisation of an era, now dead and gone, which was dominated by Fascism. The scientific evidence is no longer convincing, if indeed it ever was, for Freud's theories of the primal anguish of birth, the Oedipus complex, the notion of increasing sexual repression in culture, and the dictatorship he postulated as imposed on primordial man. Nor is it any more evident now that what characterises the relation between people is aggression. There is aggression; but there is also co-operation (the latter far more frequent than the former), and the current that alternates between them is a creative, life-producing force. Freud found it inconceivable; but even today there are primitive peoples who have never heard of war. War is in fact a relatively recent phenomenon. In one form or another, human culture has existed for at least a million years, war for only the last ten thousand years.

It is likewise hardly evident, in scientific terms, that sublimation is hopeless on the grounds that it is bound to remain restricted to the few and it cannot give complete satisfaction. This idea underestimates the potential for creativity which, in almost every human being, is present once the repressive factor has been removed. Freud wrongly interpreted man's needs as static and unchangeable. Alexander Mitscherlich, although faithful to Freud in his general pessimism, rightly points to Norbert Elias' theory of *historical change in the economy of emotional shock* in his *On the Idea of Peace and Man's Aggression (Die Idee des Friedens und die menschliche Aggressivität.*). Elias points out, in *On the Process of Civilization*, 1939, (*Uber den Prozess der Zivilisation*), that many practices which used to arouse vindictiveness now engender only revulsion. He cites as an example the sixteenth-century custom of setting fire to a dozen or so live cats on St. John's Day. 'This ceremony was widely acclaimed. It was carried out to the sound of festive music. Beneath a kind of scaffold, an enormous pyre was erected. Then a sack or basket full of cats was hung from the scaffolding. It caught fire. The cats fell into the blazing pile and were burnt, while the crowd enjoyed their mewing and screeching. The king and his household were usually present. Sometimes, the honour of igniting the pile fell to the king or the dauphin.' Now we no longer burn cats; we dance or play football instead. Our needs change. Our aggression finds different ways of expressing itself. Is it inconceivable that one day wars, like the burning of cats, will arouse universal revulsion and disappear as a phenomenon in history?

The alternation between co-operation and aggression is a dialectical unity. But there is an important difference in emphasis between this approach and that of the Marxist dialecticians. For them, the central thing is the relationship of repulsion between thesis and antithesis, between subject and object. They are inclined to fix on a single relation where there are two. The force of attraction between two 'opposing' elements is at least as essential as the force of repulsion.

For Marx, the major significance of the relation between proletariat and bourgeoisie is that it is a hostile one. The struggle between the two antagonists will create a new form of society. The attraction, the potential co-operation which also exists between the two classes is something that he abhors. It is Kropotkin's great merit that he stresses the attractive relation between two elements; and I want now to apply the relation to antagonists as well. Between ruling class and oppressed class there is a repulsive, just as there is an attractive, relationship. There is a force of attraction between our sun and its planets, but also a repellent force. The balance between these two forces makes it possible for the planets to revolve round the sun. A balance of forces has long been absent from the relation between the classes; they came into existence through a prolonged ascendency of the power of repulsion. Only the power of attraction can unite the classes and so bring them to an end. But I realise that conflict is required for the necessary force of attraction to be aroused. To that extent I agree with the Marxists that the classless society will not emerge without conflict. But neither will it come without co-operation between individuals and groups from both classes, who make use of their 'mutual attraction'. The end we want to achieve is the peaceful overthrow of authority; and I think we can do this through the force of attraction we can exert as fighters for a just and loving world. Always be aware of the attractive power that you have over your opponent. Make him recognise himself in you and come to understanding through you. Learn the fighting methods of the Marxists insofar as they accord with the end you have in view. But point out to them that because they want to utilise only the repellent relationships, they will not achieve any decisive changes; for it is the absence of any other relation – the lack of humour, provocation, 'happening' and utopianism – that makes their methods so rigid and their results to date so authoritarian. Kropotkin's symbol is the industrious and co-operative ant, Lorenz's symbol the aggressive swordfish; my symbol is the peacock-butterly. Splendidly and eagerly, this butterfly flutters about with its beautiful bright wings. Love and co-operation are its normal mode of life. If a predator approaches, it opens out its wings so that the predator is suddenly confronted with great, menacing eyes, gazing intently in its direction. And the predator retreats. In the peacock-butterly affection and aggression are one. Love and aggression, the power of attraction and of repulsion, carry it through life and death.

CHAPTER FOUR

The Marriage of Love and Creativity

Why is it that in man incest is almost universally forbidden? The anthropologist's usual reply is Malinowski's, who says that sexual relations between parents and children are thought to undermine parental authority. Such an answer is typical of the belief in authoritarian relationships as something universal, a belief which many anthropologists still hold and which they project as a solution to questions they do not understand. Lévi-Strauss's answer is more plausible. He says that the ban on incest is necessary because otherwise relations *between* families would be weakened. Marriage outside the family engenders strong ties of affection and solidarity between families, so that a whole network of interconnected families is created where there would otherwise have been only families in isolation. The widest possible choice of marriage-partner creates a homogeneous and properly blended social fabric.

What Lévi-Strauss has said supports Kropotkin's view of anthropology and history, which is based on the conviction that, in the course of his evolution, man as a rule has done whatever he could to establish co-operation. In contrast to most of his Hobbesian contemporaries, who claimed that in ancient times human beings wandered around in small, embattled family groups, looting and pillaging, Kropotkin believed that they lived in clans and avoided competition as much as possible. He alleged that the members of these clans did all they could to assist one another, as was the case with primitive tribes living in his own day. In *Mutual Aid* he describes in detail the peaceful, co-operative existence of Bushmen, Hottentots, Papuans, Australian Aboriginees,

Eskimoes, Aleutian Islanders, Boerjates, Kabyles, Caucasian mountain-dwellers, African tribes and so on.

Among the Hottentots, Kropotkin tells us, an individual who is hungry and is about to eat must first call out three times, aking whether anyone else is hungry, whereas in our society the respectable citizen has only to pay so much tax for this or that social service. Generally speaking, what prevails among these 'uncivilised' tribes is a primitive kind of communism. Kropotkin describes how under the influence of 'civilisation' private ownership is forcing its way in among them. Faced with the problem of preventing the destruction of the group's solidarity by the concentration of property in the hands of one man, the Eskimoes, for instance, have hit upon the following solution. When a man has grown rich, he invites the members of his clan to a big feast; and after they have all had a great deal to eat and drink, he divides his fortune among them. 'On the Yukon river' recounts Kropotkin (quoting from Dall's *Alaska and its Resources*), 'Dall came across a family of Aleutians that had given away in this fashion ten guns, ten complete sets of fur clothing, two hundred strings of pearls, piles of blankets, ten wolf-hides, and the pelts of two hundred beavers and five hundred sable-martens. And the members of the family afterwards took off their party clothes and gave them away too; they put on old, worn furs and addressed their kinsmen, saying that although they were now poorer than any one of them, they had won their friendship.' The custom reminds one of the Indian potlatches, by which in rather the same way hand-outs are organised and held as happenings by well-to-do people.

Since Kropotkin wrote, innumerable observational experiments have been carried out by ethnologists and anthropologists; and generally they confirm his opinion that among primitive peoples co-operation is the rule, at any rate within the context of the tribe. The African Pygmies never steal or commit murder; according to the oldest living member of the tribe, such a thing has never happened (Van den Bergh). The Manbati Pygmies of the Congo are friendly and hospitable people; they never steal from or murder one another. The Kalahari Bushmen were exterminated by the British and the

Dutch during our golden age of colonialism. But people who knew them described them to Dornan, Waitz and Elisee Reclus (a great friend of Kropotkin's) as gentle, friendly folk without central authorities or criminality.

The Veddahs of Ceylon are 'as peaceful as they could possibly be. They are proverbially truthful and honest' (Bailey). The Semang of Malaya have no form of government. 'Liberty, not licence, is the principle of the Semang group and the character of each individual! They eat communally and share their food; theft is absolutely unknown to them' (Schebesta). The Negritos of the Philippines are totally pacifist, and they welcome any member of any other tribe into their houses. When a missionary (Van den Bergh) asked whether they would consent to other Negritos from distant places coming to hunt in their woods, they replied: 'Yes, if they are fond of coming to hunt here, we are happy about that. Why not?'

The Eskimoes actually have no words for murder and theft. They do not understand what it means to say that one is a soldier. Verrill says of the North American Indians that the generally accepted idea of their savagery is a misconception, and that if a few nasty traits do appear, this is due to the influence of white men – a consequence of the armed resistance the whites forced upon them. Verrill observes: 'I have seen Indians alter the place they had chosen for their camp so as not to disturb a nesting bird.' And H.J. Massingham says of this: 'We might almost describe such delicate feelings as a fantastic kind of piety; and it is a telling criticism of our civilised mentality that we regard this sort of conduct as childish.' It was the character of the 'Redskin' that so profoundly influenced the French humanitarian thinkers of the eighteenth century and their ideas of the 'noble savage'.

The Poonan of Borneo have no class structures and no private property; they have everything in common. Fights seldom occur among them. Public opinion and tradition are the sole and sufficient sanctions for behaviour among these harmonious nomads. Each shares with each the food, animal or vegetable, that skill or fortune has brought his way.

Feuds, wars and cruelty do also occur among primitive

peoples. That there are tribes who adopt a double ethic – meaning in fact that they are friendly toward their fellow tribesmen but suspicious of strangers – is recognised by Kropotkin. He explains this in terms of superstition and ignorance. Superstition leads them into feuding. Unfamiliarity makes it impossible to identify with strangers; and that causes them to adopt a less friendly attitude toward the world outside (although federations of tribes or clans do exist, as with the Iroquois Indians). Cannibalism, Kropotkin says, arose in the first instance because of famine and has persisted subsequently because of the strength of superstition.

Superstition and lack of knowledge cannot account for all aggressiveness on the part of primitive peoples. Marx underestimated the power of attraction between thesis and antithesis. Kropotkin underestimated the force of repulsion which, whether latent or not, is always present between two elements. The alternating current of co-operation and aggression can render the differences between primitive cultures more far-reaching than Kropotkin thought. He was right insofar as co-operation is indeed a normal pattern within the tribe. But it is not true that there are no important deviations from that norm: modern anthropologists have found that the Dobuan and Utah Indians are as pathologically aggressive as the Zunji Indians are consistently co-operative, while the Arapesh of West Iran, for instance, pursue some forms of aggression and not others. As Kropotkin knew, the factor of mutual aid is not in itself sufficient to explain evolution. We must recognise that both factors together create the field of tension within which life is possible and within which we can learn to adopt some behaviour-patterns as suitable and reject others as unsuitable. We must recognise that this field of tension offers the possibility of many variants, according to whether the alternating process is making destructive or creative use of the potentialities of co-operation and aggression.

In human beings and animals, the autonomous nervous system consists of two opposed and mutually counterbalancing systems: the sympathetic and the parasympathetic. The former activates and agitates, the latter soothes and conserves. The sympathetic nervous system prepares a body for aggression. It makes a cat's hairs bristle, and in all of us it gives rise to the phenomena associated with excitement, such as high blood-pressure, accelerated heartbeat and breathing, perspiration and so on. The parasympathetic nervous system offsets all this and supplies the tranquility that ensues after fighting, love-making and other emotionally exciting activities.

I would compare aggressiveness in society with the sympathetic nervous system in the body, and co-operation in society with the parasympathetic system. Between the two systems there exists the same dual relation of attraction and repulsion which liberates either a creative or a destructive force.

In certain cultures – such as those of the Dobuan and Utah Indians, and especially western culture as it is disseminated in all its various forms throughout the world – the sympathetic nervous system of society finds itself in a state of chronic over-stimulation. The aggressive and competitive energy generated in it ensures that the effect of the alternating process is mainly destructive. Everywhere millions of young men and even women (whose nature it is to uphold the 'parasympathetic' over against the men) arm themselves under the direction of aged, professional killers, corrupt scientific maniacs and trouble-making politicians. A few succeed through keen competition in becoming extremely rich, while others a hundred miles or so away, or even in the same city, are dying of hunger.

The sympathetic nervous system is feverishly active, while the parasympathetic tries desperately to restore the balance. While American soldiers pursue their murderous activity in Vietnam and elsewhere, their contemporaries at the universities demonstrate their revulsion by unruly behaviour. While the chemical and automobile industries are busy laying waste to nature, nature-lovers and animals are trying with pathetically inadequate resources to defend it. The autonomous nervous system of western culture is gravely disturbed. There is a danger that the creative co-operation between sympathetic and parasympathetic nervous systems will be finally disrupted: because of the excessive and persistent aggressive activity of the authorities, the repulsive relation threatens to obliterate the attractive relation for good. What will happen when aggression, aroused by the sympathetic nervous system of the social organism, has had removed from it its natural check – that is, the co-operation made possible by the parasympathetic system of the same organism? Unchecked aggression will release a disconnected and destructive force which will quickly reach its goal of total destruction. Millions of species have already perished as a result of the 'alternating current' being disrupted – so why not ourselves?

To give a complete picture, I should mention as a possibility the other sort of interruption of society's autonomous nervous system. In some cultures there is such a complete absence of aggression that the parasympathetic system exercises a permanent, albeit a mild, dictatorship. In the case of races like the Pygmies the result is that their culture remains more or less the same for thousands of years. That situation is static and uncreative; but still I think that this disruption of the social nervous system is preferable to that of our own culture, because it offers many possibilities for the future; the individuals affected may be quite happy, and it does not create difficulties for other cultures.

How is it that a culture can emerge in which society's sympathetic nervous system is chronically over-strained, in which aggressiveness has much more energy than co-operation? Let us see whether Kropotkin's philosophy of history provides any answer.

War, as we have seen, is a relatively recent phenomenon. It did not really start until the rise of centrally organised states in the Middle East and elsewhere. Kropotkin goes on to say that the ancient peoples, irrespective of whether central states existed or not, developed village communities such as still exist today in large areas of the Third World. A village society is based on the common ownership of land and governmental and juridical autonomy. It forms a communal organisation of families which, had they been isolated, could not have survived. Together they can tackle the various problems with which their natural environment confronts them. As an example, Kropotkin takes the village society

(*Thaddat*) of the Kabyles, as it was in his day. During the long period of domination by Arab overlords, a law of inheritance had been imposed upon them. Although they had reverted to their tribe's traditional law, one result of the period of legalised inheritance had been that, besides the usual common ownership of land, a form of private ownership continued to exist as well. Different Kabyle villages formed a tribe, different tribes a federation; and various federations often found a yet greater whole, especially if that was desirable for joint defence. The Kabyles were strangers to any authority save that of the *djemmaa* or assembly of the village community. All males could take part in the *djemmaa*; and decisions were taken unanimously. The *djemmaa* looked after the apportioning of the corporate lands, and public works, which were usually carried out communally. Paths, small mosques, fountains, irrigation-channels, fences and so on were the business of the village community, whereas bigger roads, mosques and market-places were regarded as the business of the tribe. Each village had its smith, who worked for the community. When the ground had to be tilled, he would visit each house to repair the implements without expecting to be paid for it. The making of new ploughs was an act of piety for which no reimbursement was possible.

When a family slaughtered a sheep for its own use, the fact was made known in the streets so that pregnant women and the sick could take from it whatever they might need. If a Kabyl on his travels found himself in difficulties, another Kabyl meeting him accidentally was bound to assist him. If he did not, then the *djemmaa* to which the victim of the trouble belonged would lodge a complaint and the *djemmaa* of the defaulting person would at once give whatever compensation was due. Any stranger who arrived at a village had a right to accommodation and provision for his horses for a certain length of time. If there was a famine anywhere, all starving strangers would be taken in. Kropotkin reports that during the famine of 1867 in the district of Declys the lives of twelve thousand people were saved in that way.

The Kabyles were also familiar with the Gof, a widely ramifying association which had some of the features of the medieval guilds. Besides the mutual protection of its members, it had intellectual and political aims that could not be attained through the territorial organisation of the village, the tribe or the confederation.

Kropotkin's rather narodnik-like vision of the village community as the central core of a mutual rendering of service was later to influence Gandhi, who was an enthusiastic reader of Kropotkin. His *sarvodaya*-society (= the ideal, just society) consisted of a confederation of village communities like these. However, in contrast to Gandhi, Kropotkin saw the rise of industry and of the city not only as inevitable but as a liberation of man from many of his worries. Like Bakunin and Marx, Kropotkin saw more clearly than Gandhi that leisure is the main condition for the building of a truly humane culture.

Out of the village community there grew the free city. First there was the autonomous Greek *polis*, and after the downfall of the Roman empire – destructive as it was of all spontaneous co-operation – the medieval town, which was very largely independent of the feudal barons. In the medieval cities of Italy, and in those of almost every other European country, there developed new forms of handicraft, industry, trade and art – for instance, architecture. Kropotkin enumerates, legitimately enough, the great number of inventions we owe to the Middle Ages – a period much despised in his day as in our own: parchment and paper, printing and engraving, improved glass and steel, clocks, telescopes, the marine compass, the new-style calendar, the decimal system, algebra, geometry, chemistry, counterpoint and so forth.

What Kropotkin found most striking in the medieval city was the guilds. These were organisations, primarily of craftsmen, but also of merchants, huntsmen, farmers, priests, painters, and even of whores and hangmen. They were united by their common interests. Fraternal feelings prevailed among them. If harm befell any member of a guild, the other members had to assist him or, if he died, his relatives. The members undertook to behave in brotherly or sisterly fashion toward one another. They supported one another in good times and bad.

If a brother committed an offence, he had to answer to the

guild court, elected by the guild members themselves. Thus, as Kropotkin observes, the judges were not legal theoreticians or people representing someone else's interests, but men who knew the accused well. Having to administer their own justice meant that the guilds were self-governing institutions. 'They combined within themselves all the principal rights which the state later appropriated on behalf of its bureaucracy and its police.' In many respects the guilds resembled the autonomous anarchists' unions which during the Spanish revolution of 1936-9 kept the economy of Catalonia going in the difficult circumstances of the civil war. The medieval town, an association of small village-type centres and guilds, was a community of interests. In *Mutual Aid* Kropotkin cites the charter of the Flemish town of Aire (1188): 'All who are citizens of the town have promised and affirmed on oath they they will assist one another as brethren in all that is fitting and fair. That if any person by his words or actions do injure another, the victim thereof will not himself take his revenge, neither he nor his servants . . . he will lodge a complaint and the offender shall make good the wrong in accordance with the sentence of the twelve elected judges who shall act as arbitrators in the matter. And if after three admonitions assailant and assailed do not submit to the verdict of the arbitrators then shall they be banished from the community as an evil person and a perjurer.' Many of the things desired by radical socialists, in Kropotkin's time as well as in our own, were actually carried out in the medieval town. There were effective measures to protect the consumer. Generally speaking, labourers worked for not more than eight hours a day, sometimes even for less. The medieval ordinances of Gutenberg say: 'Everyone should find his work congenial' and 'No one is to appropriate what others have produced by industry and labour while he himself does nothing; for laws must be a shield to industry and labour . . .'

Why was the medieval township ousted by the rising national and centralist state? Kropotkin has a good answer to that. The medieval towns interpreted the idea of co-operation in too restricted a sense. The towns set out to compete with one another. Their economy was centred too much on trade and industry, so that they came to have trouble with the neglected peasants, who then began to fasten their hopes solely on the king – the more so because the cities had failed to put an end to the petty wars between members of the feudal nobility. One result of commerce was the emergence of wealthy families with small private armies that eventually gave the towns a decidedly class character. The discord and division in the towns and between the towns gave the modern state its chance. The inroads made by Turk and Mongol into Europe reinforced still further the need for a powerful state. The state stripped the guilds of their rights and their independence, and likewise did away with the common ownership of land (in France it was done eventually by Turgot in 1787, in Britain during the period 1750-1850).

As the citizens' obligations toward the state increased, so the duties and the aid they owed to one another decreased. The law of the state came to dominate everyone and everything, as the local law of custom was gradually rescinded. The wars between states entailed slaughter on a huge scale. The natural co-operation of local communities diminished under pressure from the state, which tried to take over this function in order to weaken the independence of regional areas.

Yet Kropotkin did not believe that mutual aid had ceased to exist. He could still see plentiful examples of co-operation – plentiful enough to support his belief in it as a guiding principle demanding to be put into practice. He observed it in the workers' struggle for the improvement of their living conditions against the ruling order; in the slum areas where the impoverished masses were sharing their last scraps of food, and looking after each other's children when the parents had to be away at work; in the thousands of scientific, artistic and educational associations, in sporting and social organisations, in charitable societies and above all in family life. Kropotkin's conclusion is: 'The destructive influence of the centralised state, the ideas of accommodating philosophers and sociologists who were proclaiming mutual hatred and relentless conflict as truths of science, were not able to bring about the extinction of human solidarity, which is so deeply rooted in our hearts and minds because it has been growing in us during the long period of our earlier development: what was a product of universal evolution since the earliest times could not be overwhelmed by a single phenomenon in that evolution. And the need for mutual aid and support which in recent times has taken refuge in the intimate family circle or in the slums, in the village or in the secret workers' associations, is asserting once again in our society today its right to be what it always has been: the leading factor in further progress.'

As I have said before, I do not entirely agree with Kropotkin that co-operation alone is the governing factor as regards further progress. I believe that the higher form of co-operation which is the result of the attraction between aggression and co-operation is the creative, progressive force. Kropotkin's reply to the question as to what is the historical cause of the over-stimulation of society's sympathetic nervous system is: the rise and triumph of the centralized state as the exponent of modern capitalism. This answer is right, and yet it does not altogether satisfy me. I would want to say that the triumph of the centralised state as the exponent of modern capitalism is a politico-social phenomenon, parallel to the socio-psychological cause of the over-stimulation of the sympathetic nervous system in our society. And this socio-psychological cause is the spirit of loveless creativity that has its source in the industrial imperialism with respect to nature and one's fellow human beings which marked the Renaissance and the industrial revolution of recent centuries.

The positive consequences of the revolutionary change that the Renaissance brought with it have been greatly overrated. In contrast to the co-operative free towns of the Middle Ages, it stressed the aggressiveness in man; and since then, apart from the creative effect of the modern physical sciences, man has also evinced markedly destructive tendencies, principally in the form of political, economic and mental imperialism.

Of course, life in the Middle Ages was no paradise on earth. The official church enriched itself, and under cover of the Crusades organised looting and pillaging in distant countries. The cruelty with which people were punished and tortured is something which in western civilisation is found now only in the prisons of Fascist and Stalinist countries; and even there it no longer occurs as a public spectacle. Nature rules sternly over the vale of tears. But in reaction to these sombre aspects – particularly in the later Middle Ages – there was a widespread growth of affection. There was co-operation between peasants, craftsmen and the other denizens of village communities, as well as between the people in the guilds and free towns, a feature of which Kropotkin drew attention; and many heretics, priests and primitive socialists were filled with a rare spirit of love. Even the Church's canon law enshrined co-operative ideas such as the joint ownership of chattels, a ban on usury and the anathema on profit. *Dulcissima rerum possessio communis est* – it is glorious indeed to possess things in common – said Clement of Alexandria. Only compare that with the glorification of private ownership by the Italian bankers of the Renaissance and the Reformers' stinginess! Even the medieval landowner would not have understood why it is a good thing to hoard money instead of spending it.

Throughout the Europe of the twelfth century, rebellious peasant leaders set themselves against the exuberant wealth and power of the Church. Our Tanchelijn, Endo de Stella, the Publicans, Begharden, Peter de Breuys, and the Albigenses declared themselves, like the Waldenses, in favour of the simple life of poverty that Christ and his apostles taught. I almost forgot the Bogomiles of southern Slavonia who, in face of persecution by the Roman and Byzantine churches, insisted on a life of love and humility.

In the thirteenth century the official church produced that most loving and gnome-like figure, Francis of Assisi, who kissed lepers and communicated with animals. According to Dante, Francis was wedded to Poverty who, since losing her first spouse, Jesus Christ, had been ravished by Popes and priests. Francis was an example to countless numbers of begging friars who lived the life of poverty; he concerned himself about the poor with a depth of feeling totally akin to that of the best of the later socialists.

The thinking of mystics like Meister Eckhart tended in the same direction. In order to live free from sin one has no need to castigate onself, he says, but one must allow oneself to be caught like a fish by the rod and line of God's Love. 'So say I of love, whoever becomes her prisoner bears the strongest of all fetters and yet carries a sweet burden . . . achieves more and gets further thereby than with every penance and every austerity . . . Therefore you can never conquer this foe better than with love.' And again: 'Work is love and love is God. God cherishes himself and his nature, his being and his Godhead. With the same love wherewith God loves me he loves all creatures' (Meister Eckhart). Compare this with the way Machiavelli, one of the greatest philosophers the Renaissance ever produced, extols the loveless cult of success in *The Prince*. He says that in order to succeed a ruler must give an impression of religiosity. 'But it is necessary that one be able to conceal this trait and that one be a great dissembler and hypocrite; people are so simple-minded and so ready to be subject to the need of the moment that the man who practises deceit will always find people who are prepared to let themselves be deceived. I will mention just one modern example. Alexander VI never did anything other than deceive people; he never contemplated anything else, and found every opportunity for it; no person was more ready to give assurances and to affirm them with solemn oaths, and no one has honoured them less; and yet he always had success with his trickery and deception, because he was pre-eminently well versed in this aspect of things.'

The peasant revolts against the nobility and the clergy were everywhere carried on in the name of real love and equality. The Peasants' Revolt of 1381, led by Wat Tyler in England, was wholly in line with the outlook of the Church reformer Wycliffe, who had denounced the Pope as Antichrist and taught that possessions were a consequence of sin: Jesus and the apostles had always taken as little with them as they could. How different from the attitude of Luther, who exhorted the rulers of his day to crush the rebellious peasants 'like mad dogs'. One can of course compare the medieval love-movements (including, for instance, the Hussites in Bohemia and Geert Grote in the Low Countries) with the Christian-communistic movement of the Anabaptists in the sixteenth century; but at a time when state and capital were in the ascendant, movements of that kind represented a feebler undercurrent than their medieval cognates.

It was in the Renaissance economy that the process of alienation began. In the Middle Ages people still had a habit of giving many things a name of their own: the prison dungeons, every house, every clock had its own name. In the Renaissance the thing became an anonymous product for sale – anonymous, that is, as regards its essential character: the only relation the trader had to the thing was expressed in its price. During the Middle Ages what was looked for in every thing and every event was the 'morality' that attached to it: its moral significance was the most essential thing about it. The merchants of the Renaissance period ceased to envisage events as 'happenings'. In the Renaissance economy the tendency to rationalise was taken so far that the labouring individual was regarded as a medium for the production process. Workers' organisations were gradually forbidden. For the great merchants to whom the love of work, of toil, was alien, the guilds were merely so many trammels. The specialist came along; to be universal was reserved for 'genius', the adulation of which now became popular. 'Virtù', the quality of the virile man of genius, trampled over the remains of every religious or ethical tradition. To squander time and money was now regarded as a sin; time and money had to be strictly measured out. Money had to be piled up; for that enabled God to see whether you deserved a place in Heaven. There also emerged the modern natural sciences. A wait-and-see attitude to nature was replaced by an aggressive one. Copernicus, Kepler, Galileo and Newton succeeded by means of experiments in formulating laws of nature which gave results. Although this was the best thing that the Renaissance contributed to our culture, the natural sciences soon became an instrument that was atrociously misused by the prevailing imperialistic outlook. The result of the aggressive use of those sciences was a crudely conducted war of conquest over nature. To this very day, people who insist that we listen to what nature has to say to us are regarded as naive and other-worldly. The natural sciences have been perversely used to exterminate mammals, insects, birds, fishes and forests; to defoliate trees and make harvesting impossible; to poison air, land and sea; to engage in atomic, bacteriological and chemical warfare.

With the Renaissance there began a story of loveless creativity which is reaching its climax in the twentieth century. Either the misuse of the natural sciences will bear us towards final destruction, or we will marshal the revolutionary power to use them to create global well-being, a 'Kabouter city' based on love and understanding. I must admit that 'Provo' should have put the emphasis more on love than on creativity; for there is much more need at the moment for the first than for the second. 'Provo' has been too much the child of the cult of creativity born in the Renaissance. Creativity by itself makes itself impossible, in the end; detached, loveless creativity is destructive. Creativity is the result of the alternating flow between co-operation and aggression; when all the energy flows onesidedly toward the pole of aggression, the result is a short-circuit.

Medieval man's wait-and-see attitude to nature is unproductive; the aggressive attitude of Renaissance man towards nature vitiates the products. It is not only the vertical, sympathetic, creative man, but also the horizontal, parasympathetic, loving man who is needed; and they must be united in the same people. Only a real marriage between aggression and co-operation, between receptiveness and activity, between creativity and love can provide us with a way forward, a way towards the true freedom which is nothing less than every man's creative participation in universal solidarity and love.

CHAPTER FIVE

Towards a New Moral Revolution

While co-operation and aggression sometimes operate in harmony by complementing and stimulating each other, they can also actively conflict by repelling each other and arresting each other's progress. Out of this interchange, this fluctuating activity, arises the energy that enables human beings to build their culture and animals to support their natural existence. Again, while sympathetic and parasympathetic nervous systems sometimes function in harmony by the complementary way in which they respectively activate and calm the bodily organs, at other times they work in mutual opposition by hindering and counteracting one another's functions. It is because of this interplay that human organs are controllable. Implicit in these analogous processes is the notion of cybernetics, which I see as being applicable to everything that we have been considering so far.

What is cybernetics? It is the 'skill' or science of *control*, based on the principle of counteraction. Everything that lives is permeated by this cybernetic principle. Take for instance a cyclist. He follows a particular route that he has chosen, and in so doing makes use of a vehicle the control of which is essential in this context. How does he succeed, despite all sorts of disruptive influences from outside – such as traffic, conflicting bodily impulses, wind and so on – in actually following his route? By steering, by exercising constant control. When a gust of wind comes from the left, he notices a deviation of the cycle to the right and he turns the handlebars to the left so as to correct the deviation. If the disturbing influence comes from the right, with a consequent deviation to the left, then in order to maintain his direction he turns the handlebars to the right.

The compensatory movements that the cyclist makes with the handlebars to traverse the route he has proposed to himself are described in the terminology of cybernetics as *counteraction.* The function of such a counteraction is to maintain a norm by offsetting or counterbalancing disruptive influences which threaten that norm. A counteraction stabilises a dynamic equilibrium within an organism and thus maintains the norm of the organism.

In the example of the cyclist the norm is the selected route. A dynamic equilibrium is involved, because using the pedals releases a force which puts cycle and cyclist in motion and keeps them in a state of balance. Counteractions function now as a brake (in this example literally), now as a stimulus. Counteractions are one element in a circular process. The movement proceeds from the cyclist (*A*) on the road, who *via* his eyes and brain (*B*) gets the data informing him to turn his handlebars (*C*) in order to correct a deviation. The cyclist (*A*) then has a look at what he has done and the circular process starts again. It can be summed up in the following diagram, taken, with a small alteration, from S.T. Bok, *Cybernetika*:

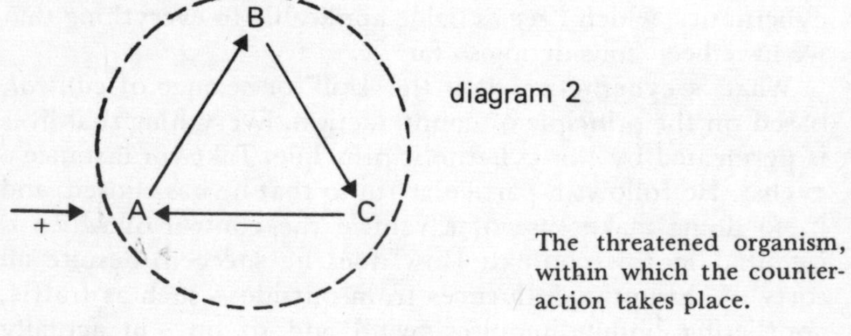

The threatened organism, within which the counteraction takes place.

The plus sign stands for the disruptive influence, the threat which sets the process in operation; and the minus sign stands for the counteraction which more or less nullifies the disruption. The cybernetic principle is not just something confined to a small number of functions. Man and woman, sympathetic and parasympathetic nervous systems, health and disease, order and disorder, town and country, specialism and general education, the young and the elderly, nomadic and sedentary populations, culture and nature – all stimulate and impede each other by turns. Man's thinking is carried out so completely within the framework of the cybernetic system that the machines we create, being faithful replicas of ourselves, are all based on the counteractional process. Bok even believes that counteraction is a typical feature of life, in view of the fact that it has not so far been observed in lifeless nature. In my view co-operation and aggression are also a cybernetic pair. They are the 'steering mechanism' of the vehicle wherewith men and animals make their way through life. Let us return for a moment to the diagram. I am going to modify it a little now in order to clarify the image of the steering and the roadway.

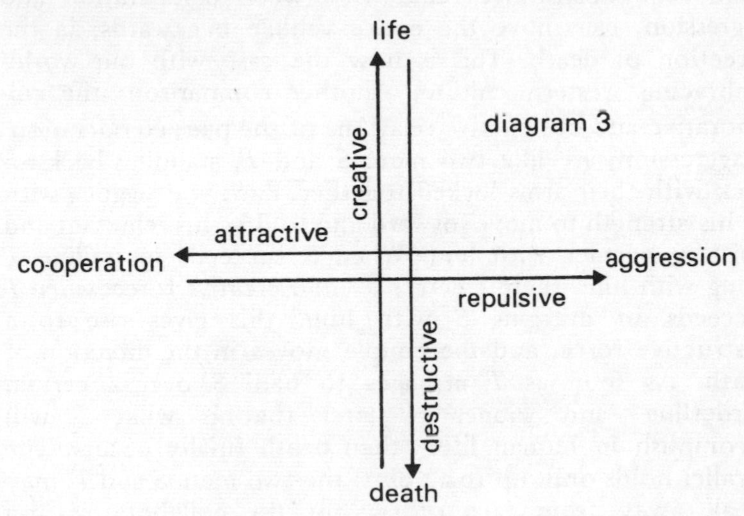

Creative and destructive energy, generated by the alternating flow between aggression and co-operation, are represented by the long arrows; these stand for the road of life. Life and death are likewise a cybernetic pair. At one moment the phenomenon of death and our awareness of it stimulate the intensity of life, at another they act as a drag upon life through the trouble and misery that they bring, and eventually put an end to it. I called the cybernetic pair, co-operation – aggression, the steering mechanism of the vehicle that carries us along the road of life. It would be better to say that it is the actual vehicle, of which the steering is an essential component.

The higher form of co-operation, or concerted activity between co-operation and aggression (the uppermost of the two arrows in the diagram), is in fact the steering; that together with the obstructive relation between co-operation and aggression (the lower arrow) constitutes our vehicle. No vehicle can move purposefully without a brake. This need is met by the obstructive relation. Moreover, the aggressive energy produced by this relation provides the vehicle with a dynamic which makes possible a variety of speeds ('aggressive' comes from the Latin *aggredi*, which in its primary sense means 'to go forward'). The higher form of aggression, which yields the obstructive relation between co-operation and aggression, can move the entire vehicle backwards, in the direction of death. This is now the case with our world-embracing western culture. Another comparison: the collaborative and obstructive relations of the pair, co-operation – aggression, are like two men, *S* and *T*, standing back-to-back with their arms locked together. Each is struggling with all his strength to move forward and to drag his reluctant and resisting partner with him. When *S* succeeds in pulling *T* along with him, there emerges a vital, creative force. when *T* succeeds in dragging *S* with him, this gives rise to a destructive force, and the couple moves in the direction of death. As soon as *T* manages to haul *S* over a certain borderline – and sooner or later that is what *T* will accomplish in human life – then death finally occurs. The parallel holds only up to a point: the two men, *S* and *T*, may break away from each other; but the collaborative and obstructive relations can never do that, because a disconnected, unrestrained force would then break loose.

Let us now forget this image. Once more, the vehicle of western civilisation is the whole play of forces arising from the interaction between co-operation and aggression. Will this vehicle manage to keep up its route, that is, towards the good fortune and happiness of those human beings who live within the culture?

If it is a living organism that functions as the cyclist in Diagram 2, it can maintain itself. If in Diagram 2 western culture is represented by *A*, which threatens to be knocked off its course by a disruptive influence (deriving from its own or from other cultures), then that danger will be noticed by scientists, journalists, people gifted with intuition and others (the information-centre comparable with the eyes and brain of the cyclist), who register the danger and make it known *via* the information-media *B*. Thereupon, people reverse the steering control *C* (which chooses aggressive or co-operative modes of conduct) and the counteractional effect that results (indicated by a minus sign in Diagram 2) neutralises the threat (+). In the current situation, this means that the steering control must be pushed over by us – the provotariat, intellectuals, workers in western culture – in a co-operative direction. There are primitive societies, like that of the Pygmies, in which aggression and competition seem scarcely to exist; and the result is a very static society indeed. A counteraction that would release the competitive feelings of the Pygmies could soon motivate their society to bring this rigidity to an end – although aggression and competition are so preponderant in the world around them that there is little need for a counteraction of this sort.

The development of the social organism is also steered by counteractions. Even so, counteractions can never totally eliminate threatening situations. Impending deviations from the norm are reduced by counteractions to a certain proportion of their original number. If the counteraction is proportional, then the part left over is a fixed percentage of the impending deviation. That is why the play of counter-actions can never come to an end. The remainder of the threat, which *does* become a reality, will invariably prove an occasion for the emergence of new threats that can be succeeded by counteractions to infinity. That this counter-actional cycle has not yet been set going in some primitive cultures calls for an explanation. I am not in a position to provide this in any detail; but I would seek it along the lines of a complete neutralisation of the tension between aggres-sive and co-operate forces, as a result of which these cultures continue to revolve in the same place around their axis. What takes over then is a total dictatorship of custom, the danger of which Kropotkin did not fully realise when he cried up the law of custom as against the law of the state. As it develops, a culture gives rise to class antagonisms. This is brought on by the scarcity of the goods that have to be distributed. The tension between the ruling and proletarian classes is one more example of a cybernetic pair activating a culture and keeping it on the move over a long period. On the one hand, the proletarian class stimulates the ruling class to greater exertions by threatening it; on the other, it checks it by extorting concessions in the form of cultural assets and liberties. The converse is equally true.

Nevertheless, every culture aims at removing our counter-balancing class antagonism, just as we strive to bring aggression and co-operation into harmony with each other. The sharpness of class antagonisms reflects the disruptive influences at work on the culture. Should we manage to develop through our culture a counteractional technique which can more or less neutralise this disruption, then the class tensions may to that extent diminish. The resistance to the threat resides in the organism itself; the counteraction to the perversions of the culture resides in that culture. It may sound utopian now; but one day it will prove possible more or less to eliminate class antagonisms. Only it will not be possible to eliminate class tensions entirely, and bring aggression and co-operation into complete harmony, because that would remove in advance the cause of further movement. The counteraction should never be allowed to obviate the threat *in toto*. In the present emergency, mankind is not assured of the remedial counteraction that will avert the threat of atomic war and large-scale famine. A fatal conjunction is a very real possibility. These conjunctions occur when the information-apparatus at the disposal of an organism does not adequately process its information and therefore does not transfer it in the right form to other organs. In that case, the response to the threat is not a counterbalancing movement (counteraction) but on the contrary a movement (conjunction) further reinforcing the effect of the threat. It is possible that the aggressive dictatorships which threatened the world during the second quarter of the twentieth century match in this way with the even more perverse dictatorship of the imperialistic world powers. However, I am more inclined to see the Cold War, the vicious policies of domination pursued by America and Russia, and the crises in the Middle East, as the aftermath of Fascism, Stalinism and imperialism than as an autonomous conjunction.

Not without reason, Desmond Morris, in *The Naked Ape*, is inclined to be pessimistic. The co-operation which he too notes as existing in considerable measure among men and animals is in danger of being made to serve the ends of the prevailing aggression. People still plunge into war, says Morris, simply in order to aid their compatriots, and not so much out of hostility toward their antagonist. Kropotkin had already observed how intense co-operation becomes behind the front in time of war. At such times, co-operation gives the appearance of being a principle even more fateful than aggression itself. Without the co-operation behind the front, the aggression could never result in such large-scale, organised carnage. I think an international co-operative counteraction is taking place that had its beginnings in the Sixties. The constellation can change and move in the opposite direction: aggression will come to the support of co-operation. Co-operation between states, groups and individuals will be strengthened by an awareness of the danger from the wretched consequences of modern nuclear aggression and a total poisoning of the environment. Mutual aid may prove resilient enough to turn an impending disaster into its opposite. Only two ways are open to us: the way to destruction or the way to freedom. Aggression implies choosing the former, and as this becomes more and more generally realised, so does the likelihood of a co-operative counteraction grow. Our information is not yet so distorted that a conjunction is inevitable; we know what is afoot and we can still react to it. The right counteraction is not going to happen of itself, as though it were our appointed destiny. The counteraction will only come if we – you and I, all of use – throw ourselves whole-heartedly and spontaneously into the struggle as counteractors, at the same time remaining clear-headed and aware of what we are doing. *If*. Thousands of species, after all, have vanished into the dark of evolution because they could not find the energy to counteract – they did not have the necessary self-knowledge. In what political forms must human co-operation express itself to be really and truly a revolutionary counteraction? Here again, in broad outline, Kropotkin has shown us the way. For co-operation *within* nations it is necessary to abolish the central organs of coercion. The organisational work must be carried out by co-operative regional councils, elected directly by the local population. They must run the economy in consultation with councils composed of representatives of factories and consumer organisations. University and school councils must organize education. Public order must be guaranteed, insofar as that might be necessary, by the appropriate local services, who are to be replaced at regular intervals and made strictly answerable to local people's councils. The same applies to the judiciary, which must see itself primarily as a healer of the symptoms of disease in society, and should therefore consist mainly of social psychologists, social psychiatrists, criminologists and other social workers.

Co-operation within states, which of course are really not states at all in the old sense but national networks of elected and regularly re-elected councils, must become the extension of all national networks into a worldwide network of complexes of representative councils with a single international world council as its centre – unity in infinite variety. For this the concept of the United Nations may serve as a starting-point. The international world council can be subdivided into economic, scientific, educational, juridical and other world councils, which would regulate global policy on a basis of mutual (and especially economic) aid. Only a revolutionary solution of this sort will suffice to put an end to extreme economic disparities, the threat of military action on this side or that, 'conventional' wars and the general danger of a totally devastating Third World War.

The age of poker-game politics is over. It led to nothing but war, dictatorships and pseudo-democracy. 'Freedom', as Marcuse has rightly said, 'is only possible as a realisation of what at the present time we still refer to as utopia.' Modern technology, allied to man's co-operative genius, could in fact realise any sort of utopia in a very short time. In the past, utopia was prevented by an economic deficiency, which was partly the result of inappropriate aggressiveness, and in its turn gave rise to a surplus of that aggressive urge. The dissemination of this insight could be one of the items of information that will furnish the self-knowledge required for the potential co-operative counteraction.

I regard the theory of cybernetics as a development of dialectics. Both offer a model for thinking that explains the evolution of an organism in terms of the tension between two poles. In dialectics, the tension between thesis and antithesis creates the synthesis; in cybernetics, the tension between threat and counteraction creates a stable equilibrium capable of sustaining a norm. Both models of evolution can be represented as spirals. The synthesis is the elevation of the original thesis into a new thesis which is in itself a new source of tension, that is to say, is bound to evoke a new antithesis. Admittedly, threat and counteraction maintain the norm of an organism, but by their polarised interaction they keep creating the organism anew. Subject and object are mutually dependent on each other for their 'metabolism'. The subject can know itself only *via* the object. Or as Hegel puts it: 'Only through the servant does the master stand in a relation with objective reality.' In both systems of thinking, the (apparent) opposites form a total unity, which again itself constitutes an opposite to another pairing of opposites. In both systems there is both an attractive and a repellent relation between the poles.

The difference between cybernetics and dialectics is that cybernetics would seem to be a model for thinking created to explain evolutionary processes, dialectics on the other hand to explain revolutionary ones. Cybernetics is a system that enables us to understand the persistence of a stable equilibrium. But how is a sudden revolution, a violent jump possible?

Let us take as an example the *ancien régime* in the Russia of 1917. That was an immense organism, keeping itself in being by means of counteractions, containing within it a vast world of component elements counteractional of themselves and counteractional in regard to one another. Just as in every society conjunctions regularly occur of organisms which perish because they are no longer able to maintain their norm, so it happened then. A sufficiently stable society is equal to it and can cope with it: if a few shops and businesses go bankrupt or people lose a little confidence in the government, that does not signal immediate revolution. But during the *ancien régime* in the final years before the revolution, too many and too essential conjunctions began to occur. Tsarism was not proof against the combined conjunctions of war, hunger, disorder, discontent, strikes, mutiny and revolutionary feeling. To ask about revolution is therefore to ask about the emergence of a conjunction. We know that conjunctions are the result of an organism's being wrongly informed about itself, or in other words the consequence of a faulty self-awareness. (The simple lesson of cybernetics is 'Know yourself! Look what you're doing!'). In the example we have chosen, this means that the Tsarist authorities had ceased to be keenly aware of what was going on within their empire, were no longer able to take effective action and so lost control of the steering. For, like all rulers, they started from the assumption that society must *be* controlled, whereas cybernetics, like anarchism, teaches us that a healthy organism controls itself. The vital factor in any revolution, therefore, is the moment when correct information changes into false or faulty information. This reversal is the 'dialectical moment', the great leap, which can no more be exactly calculated than the moment when a man who has been slowly losing his hair can all of a sudden be described as 'bald'. This discontinuity has to be accounted for in terms of the obstructive or opposing relation between thesis and antithesis, which is, as I see it, the primary concern of dialectical philosophy. A continuous process like a cyclist's ride can hardly be explained by the dialectical mode of thinking, in which the accent falls on revolutionary moments. In the light of dialectics, what is continuous can only be viewed as a constituent part of a discontinuous process. Cybernetics can offer an excellent account of the continuity of a process by applying the co-operative relation between threat and counteraction.

Thus the two systems are complementary. Dialectics can account for historical leaps within the framework of a continuous evolution; cybernetics explains the continuity of events within the framework of a discontinuous revolution. Taken together, they are able to give us an insight into the single continuous-discontinuous metabolic process of living.

Before I try, as a conclusion to this little book, to show why Kropotkin's philosophy is the germ of an approach to things that gives occasion for a conditional optimism, I must first say that Kropotkin had no feeling for dialectics. As a convinced positivist, who tries to arrive at a synthesised world view by putting together the results of all the sciences, he could only regard dialectics as a new kind of metaphysics. That would also be his verdict, I am quite sure, on the philosophy I have been outlining here. But I would like to emphasise again that it is he and no one else who has made this sort of outlook possible by giving first place, in such an irrefutable and scientific way, to the principle of mutual aid, of the attractive relation between two elements. Kropotkin's application of the mutual aid principle is too restricted; for he applied it only to individuals and groups, not to alternative modes of behaviour like aggression and co-operation and other apparent opposites. But it is precisely through the application of mutual aid to these, and also to the pairing – quite unknown to him – of threat and counter-action, that a cybernetic-cum-dialectical model of evolution becomes possible: a model that can provide us with many insights and can thus help us to prevent the destruction of our species.

What counteraction is it that has enabled us till now to prevent the outbreak of a Third World War? We have succeeded thus far through mutual fear and a tentative start with mutual aid. At the end of the day this counteraction is inadequate. It allows the same threat to continue, and stimulates rather than resolves it. In the long run, only mutual aid of a thoroughgoing kind between individuals and peoples is an appropriate counteraction. For when everything is threatened with destruction, the only commensurate counteraction is that everything should function in concert. During recent decades the workers of western Europe have been through a sorry process of development from vanguard of revolution to rearguard of exploitation – and that on a world scale. All of us profit from the advantages we enjoy at the expense of the proletarians of the Third World. But a new insurgent class has arisen; and this provotariat of students and other unencapsulated young people can serve to being about a counteraction which is both necessary and logically to be expected. In the past five years they have made a very promising start with this. The western world, as well as eastern Europe and Japan, are experiencing the desired counteraction as it begins to get under way. The aggression in this world is now meeting with a certain response. Students are demanding project-schooling, which is to say, co-operation, and no compartmentalised idiots, which is to say, no blind aggression. They are demanding an educational system in which people arrive at understanding through a process of give and take and not by means of authoritarian suggestion. When these ideas have been realised inside the universities (and that is inevitable), then they cannot fail to exercise a powerful influence for change on businesses, factories and organisations outside the universities; for in a technological society higher education is a vital organ. It is already clear that students are no isolated elite. 'Nearly thirty per cent of those who took over the Maagdenhuis', the right wing papers plaintively disclosed, 'were not students'. A part of the latest generation of workers is no longer to be kept happy and content with material well-being. My optimism is provisional because the necessary counteraction will only come if we really become counteractional 'kabouters' in the culture. We must become kabouters, gnomes, again because we must once more begin to feel that we are bound up with nature. The industrial revolution has estranged us from nature. We have become creatures of culture who believe that we have to subdue nature. The subtle fantasy that dominated the thought-world of medieval man has been suppressed by the rationalistic and utilitarian considerations of industrial society. I do not want to return to the Middle Ages, but on the contrary to take a step toward the future. I want to set free in us, after five centuries of incarceration, the medieval kabouter of nature and endow him with all the rich creativeness of modern thinking. The condition for optimism about the future is that the modern kabouter become a 'playful technologist', linked with nature.

As a kabouter of culture, he must be counteractional, because he will only have a future if he creates it for himself, by engendering a co-operative and playful counteraction to the aggressive and utilitarian spirit of the industrial age. Such a counteraction implies nothing less than the making of a political, economic, social, educative, technological and moral revolution. I believe that the possibility of this has become evident from the actions of the provotariat in the wealthy countries and the proletariat in the poor countries during the Sixties. The coming of the counteractional kabouter of culture is presaged by the revolt of the provotariat.

The modern kabouter not only effects a revolutionary counteraction in the world outside; he also carries the cybernetic principle within him. He knows himself in all his conflicts and contradictions and is able to use every possibility they provide. The culture-kabouter's communication is a permanent circulatory process, not only between himself and the external world, but also between one of his I's and the other. He is not only playful, but useful. If he is a woman, she displays manlike traits. If he is a man, he will also behave like a woman, because while the unity grows more and more intense, he will also experience the contrast with greater and greater intensity. Although he may be a townsman, his interest and concern will go out to the countryside. Although he may be a traveller, he will want for a time to live somewhere. Although universal, he will have his special skills and interests. Although playful as a child, none the less the wisdom of an old man will be his. Although he will be concentrated on himself, he will be a declared altruist. In everything he is a practised novice, a professional amateur. Although a political agitator, he cannot do without quiet and intimacy. Thanks to his skill in getting contraries to co-operate, he knows how to steer his liberated society, the 'kabouter city', and no longer to rule it.

Kropotkin was a modern culture-kabouter, prematurely born. He was an urbagrarian, resident nomad, practical theorist, intellectual gardener, altruistic egoist, level-headed agitator, scientific utopian. The new, long-haired anarchism should be accompanied by the appearance of many individual, counteractional culture-kabouters. It is up to us to make this possibility come true. The day may come when Israeli and Arab, like ants from a single human tribe, will eat the honey out of each other's mouths.